GENETIC ENGINEERING
THE FACTS

Sally Morgan

Evans

Evans Brothers Limited

Published by
Evans Brothers Limited
2A Portman Mansions
Chiltern Street
London W1U 6NR

Reprinted 2006

Consultants: Professor Derek Burke
             Professor Michael Lipton
             Nuffield Council of Bioethics
Editor: Su Swallow
Design: Neil Sayer

First published in paperback in 2003 by
Evans Brothers Limited
©Evans Brothers Limited 2001

British library Cataloguing in Publication Data

Morgan, Sally
  Genetic engineering : the facts
  1.Genetic engineering - Moral and ethical aspects -
Juvenile literature
  I.Title
  174.2'5

ISBN 0237524848

Printed in China through Colorcraft Limited, Hong
Kong

VISIT OUR WEBSITE
www.evansbooks.co.uk

ACKNOWLEDGEMENTS

For permission to reproduce copyright material, the author and publishers gratefully acknowledge the following:

cover Ecoscene/Sally Morgan **contents** Ecoscene/Robin Williams **page 6 – 7** Ecoscene/Alan Towse **page 9** J.C.Revy/Science Photo Library Prof.K.Seddon & Dr.T.Evans/Queen's University Belfast/Science Photo Library **page 11** David Parker/Science Photo Library **page 12** Robert Harding Picture Library **page 13** Adam Hart-Davis/Science Photo Library **page 14** Robert Harding Picture Library **page 15** Ecoscene/Angela Hampton **page 16** James Holmes/Celltech Ltd/Science Photo Library **page 17** Mark Clarke/ Science Photo Library **page 18** CC Studio/Science Photo Library **page 19** Weiss/Jerrican/Science Photo Library **page 20** Geoff Tompkinson/Science Photo Library **page 21** PA News Photo Library **page 22** Ecoscene/Andrew Brown **page 23** Ecoscene/Andy Hibbert (right) Ecoscene/Erik Schaffer (left) **page 24** Ecoscene/Kevin King (top) Jonathan Smith/Sylvia Cordaiy Photo Library (bottom) **page 25** Ecoscene/Norman Rout **page 27** Ecoscene/Joel Creed **page 29** Ecoscene/ Mike Maidment **page 30** Ecoscene/Wayne Lawler **page 34** Ecoscene/Andrew Brown **page 35** Ecoscene/Alan Towse (left) Charles & Sandra Hood/Bruce Coleman Ltd (right) **page 36** Rosenfeld Images Ltd/Science Photo Library **page 37** Ecoscene **page 38** Ecoscene/Angela Hampton **page 40** Ecoscene/McHugh **page 41** Ecoscene/McHugh **page 43:** Ecoscene/Alan Towse **page 45** Ecoscene/Frank Blackburn **page 47** Ecoscene/Andrew Brown **page 48** Ecoscene/Quentin Bates **page 50** Ecoscene/Robin Williams **page 51** Ecoscene/Chinch Gryniewicz **page 52** Ecoscene/R. Greenwood **page 53** Ecoscene/David Wootton **page 54** Ecoscene/Chinch Gryniewicz **page 55** Ecoscene/W.Lawler **page 56** Rosenfeld Images Ltd/Science Photo Library **page 57** Ecoscene/ Beavis **page 59** Ecoscene/Sally Morgan **page 60** Chris Priest/Science Photo Library **page 61** J.C.Revy/Science Photo Library **page 62** Ecoscene/Robin Redfern **page 63** Peter Menzel/Science Photo Library **page 64** Ecoscene/Chinch Gryniewicz **page 66** Dr Gopal Murti/Science Photo Library **page 67** Geoff Tompkinson/Science Photo Library **page 68** Topham Picturepoint **page 70** Barros & Barros/Image Bank (top) Li Ken Ai/Image Bank (bottom) **page 72** Klaus Guldbrandsen/Science Photo Library **page 73** James Stevenson/Science Photo Library **page 77** Alan Gould/A-Z Botanical Collection Ltd **page 79** Topham Picturepoint **page 81** Ecoscene/L.A.Raman **page 84** Press Association/Topham **page 86** Press Association/Topham

Text by Professor Derek Burke, pages 84-87, reproduced with permission from *Feedback*, the quarterly magazine of the Food and Drink Federation.
The Prince of Wales's ten questions on genetic engineering, pages 84-87, reproduced with permission of HRH The Princes of Wales's Office.

CONTENTS

Introduction —

> I have absolutely no anxiety. I am worried about a lot of things, but not about modified food.
>
> Dr James Watson,
> Nobel prize winner for his work
> with Francis Crick on DNA

Bioscience is our future

You say tomato... I say genetic nightmare

Protesters destroying a field of GM oil seed rape which was part of a crop trial.

Genetic engineering, we are told, will allow us to produce 'designer' babies, to feed the world and prolong life indefinitely. It will help us to clean up our environment. There will be new drugs to cure diseases. Scientists recently succeeded in designing and building a form of life itself.

Such developments raise many ethical and social questions about human health, the environment, animal welfare and agriculture. Will unrestricted genetic manipulation destroy biodiversity? What are the long-term effects of eating genetically modified food? How do we control research on human genes? Who owns the rights to

GM food – a politi

act or fiction?

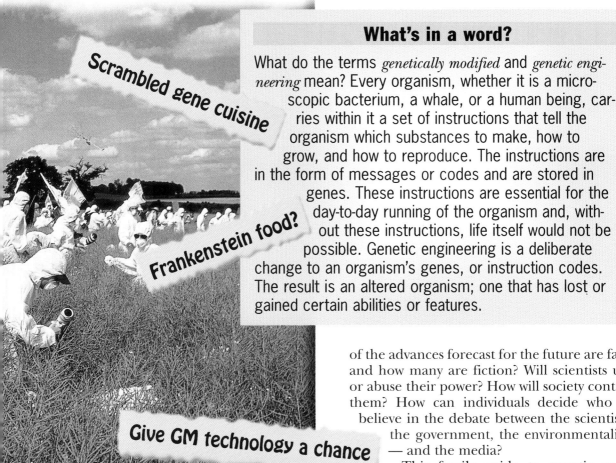

Scrambled gene cuisine

Frankenstein food?

Give GM technology a chance

t potato

What's in a word?

What do the terms *genetically modified* and *genetic engineering* mean? Every organism, whether it is a microscopic bacterium, a whale, or a human being, carries within it a set of instructions that tell the organism which substances to make, how to grow, and how to reproduce. The instructions are in the form of messages or codes and are stored in genes. These instructions are essential for the day-to-day running of the organism and, without these instructions, life itself would not be possible. Genetic engineering is a deliberate change to an organism's genes, or instruction codes. The result is an altered organism; one that has lost or gained certain abilities or features.

of the advances forecast for the future are fact, and how many are fiction? Will scientists use or abuse their power? How will society control them? How can individuals decide who to believe in the debate between the scientists, the government, the environmentalists — and the media?

This family guide to genetic engineering will give you the facts and allow you to make your own, informed decisions about the key issues raised by the advances of biotechnology.

altered genes and animals?

There seems little doubt that our future will, in many ways, be shaped by genetic engineers. Genetically engineered foods and life-saving drugs are already in widespread use, and many more genetically engineered plants and animals are being developed. But how many

Genetic modification takes mankind into realms that belong to God and God alone.

HRH Prince Charles, 1998

1. What's in a gene?

Gene technology is the basis of the new biotechnology industry. In order to understand what is going on in the field of genetic engineering, it is necessary to know some basic biological facts about cells, and the genes that are found within them.

All organisms, whether plant or animal, need a set of instructions in order to be able to function properly. These instructions are found in almost every cell. They tell a cell what materials to make, how to grow, when to divide, and how to repair itself — in fact, how to perform every process that goes on in the cell. The instructions are inherited from the cell's parents, and are held as a code that is stored in the genetic material of the cell.

Cell secrets

Complex organisms such as humans are made up of millions of cells. The control centre of the cell is the nucleus. It is here that the genetic material — chromosomes — is found. A single chromosome is a very long, thin strand made of a substance called DNA. The number of chromosomes in a cell is characteristic to each organism. For example, a human has 46, a locust has 22, while a crocus has only six.

Most human cells contain 46 chromosomes, 23 inherited from the mother and 23 from the father. The sex cells, eggs in the female and sperm in the male, have only 23 chromosomes each. When an egg and sperm fuse at

If all the DNA in just one human were stretched out, it would reach to the Sun and back 50 times.

fertilisation, the new cell regains the normal number of 46 chromosomes.

A chromosome is sub-divided into genes. A single chromosome can carry many hundreds of genes. There are around 40,000 different genes, each with a specific job in a human cell. So far, we only know the job of a few hundred genes but, within the near future, scientists will know the position and role of every single one.

DNA is a huge, coiled molecule; so long that, if the DNA from one human cell was stretched out, it would be one metre in length. If all the DNA in just one human were stretched out, it would reach to the Sun and back 50 times.

Gene control

Much of an animal's body is made of protein. Proteins are essential, as they are one of the body's vital building blocks. There are many different types

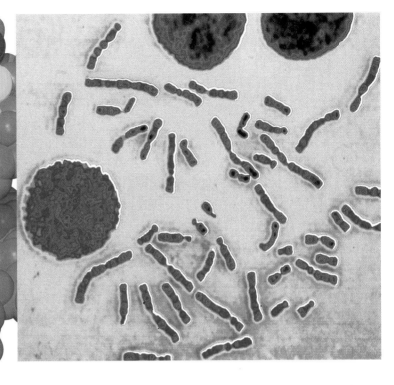

(Above) nuclei and strand-like chromosomes of a male. Chromosomes are only visible during cell division. Each chromosome has a characteristic length and appearance, some being much shorter than others. (Left) DNA, which is actually made of two strands twisted together in a spiral called a helix. It is rather like a twisted ladder, where the sides are made from sugar and phosphate molecules. They alternate with each other: sugar — phosphate — sugar. The rungs of the ladder are formed by a link between molecules called bases. It is the order of bases on a strand of DNA that forms the genetic code.

> ' **DNA neither knows nor cares. DNA just is. And we dance to its music.**
>
> Richard Dawkins, Charles Simonyi Professor of the Public Understanding of Science at Oxford University and author of *The Selfish Gene*, 1998 '

of protein, but they are all made from amino acids. There are just 20 different amino acids, but hundreds of amino acids are joined together in a chain to form a single protein. It is the order in which the amino acids are arranged that determines the type of protein. One particularly important group of proteins are the enzymes. These are biological catalysts, and they make chemical reactions in cells work faster. Without enzymes, the body would be unable to function correctly. For example, the enzyme salivary amylase is found in saliva, where its job is to break starch down into sugar.

Genes control protein manufacture in the cell. A different gene controls the manufacture of each protein. For example, only a few genes code for the blood groups, while another is responsible for making the brown pigment in skin, hair and eyes; one gene codes for the protein haemoglobin, which is found in red blood cells, while another codes for insulin, the hormone that

A handbook of human life

One of the most ambitious biological projects ever undertaken was started in 1990. It is the human genome project, which aims to map all of the human DNA, the genome being the complete set of genetic information contained within a cell. The task is enormous, because the DNA in the human cell contains 3,000 million DNA base pairs on its chromosomes.

The project, which involves scientists from all around the world, will soon be complete. The first stage is to map the genome; that is, to find the position of all the genes on human chromosomes. This is not an easy task, for the genes only make up five per cent of the DNA. They are separated by long lengths of non-functional DNA — nicknamed junk DNA. The second stage is to discover the sequence of bases that make up each gene. In the long term, the scientists aim to sequence all the DNA, including the junk DNA, as this is useful to evolutionary biologists. Chromosome 22, the smallest chromosome in the body, was the first to have its code deciphered.

By the time the project is complete, we will know the position and genetic code for every gene in the human body. It will be a 'handbook of human life'. With this information, it would be possible to alter human DNA and carry out highly sophisticated genetic engineering on human beings. It will significantly increase our understanding of the workings of the human body and aid in the diagnosis and treatment of genetic diseases.

A robot arm loads DNA on to plastic plates in an automated laboratory dedicated to mapping the human genome. In December 1999, an international team of researchers achieved a scientific milestone by unravelling for the first time the genetic code of an entire human chromosome. They deciphered the sequence of 33.5 million 'letters', or chemical components, that make up the DNA of chromosome 22.

> To see the entire sequence of a human chromosome for the first time is like seeing an ocean liner emerge out of the fog, when all you've seen before were row boats.
>
> Dr Francis Collins, Director of the National Human Genome Research Institute

Children inherit their genes from their parents. The new combination of genes produces a child who may resemble its parents, but has new characteristics as well.

regulates the level of glucose in the blood. If the gene is altered in some way, or damaged, it may not be able to make the protein, and the body may suffer from a malfunction. A single faulty gene, for example, causes the disease cystic fibrosis. The gene is said to have mutated or changed.

Parent power

A person's appearance tells us something about the genes he or she carries. There are two genes for each characteristic in each cell, one inherited from the father and the other from the mother. Genes can exist in two forms, dominant and recessive. For example, the gene for brown eyes is dominant, while the gene for blue or grey is recessive. A brown-eyed person must carry at least one gene for brown eyes. The brown dominant gene will always mask the presence of the recessive gene. But a person with blue or grey eyes will definitely have two recessive genes.

Each new individual inherits all its genetic characteristics from its parents. The mixture of characteristics, and the fact that some dominant genes may mask recessive ones, produces variation, and makes us all different from one another. Although we are all human beings, and belong to the same species, there are enough small differences between us to recognise one another as different individuals. All species have this variation. Plants of the same species, for example, may differ in leaf length and petal colour.

Genotype and phenotype

The term 'genotype' is used to describe the genetic makeup of an organism. Phenotype refers to the appearance of an individual and it results from an interaction between the individual's genotype and the effect of the environment. For example, identical twins will have the same genetic make-up or genotype, but their appearance can be affected by their environment as well. They may have different diets or live in different parts of the world. A stunted oak tree surviving between rocks on a mountain side will look very different to an oak tree growing in a sheltered valley. An individual's colour, shape, behaviour and even sex can be influenced by its environment. For example, some reptile eggs if incubated at higher than normal temperatures hatch as females. This is due in part to gene expression, when a gene operates under some circumstances but not others.

Natural selection

The individual characteristics of an organism affect its ability to survive and to breed. An individual with an advantageous characteristic, such as disease resistance, is more likely to survive and to produce more offspring. In time, these characteristics become more common. They have been selected for. Any disadvantageous characteristic will be selected against. If these selection processes continue

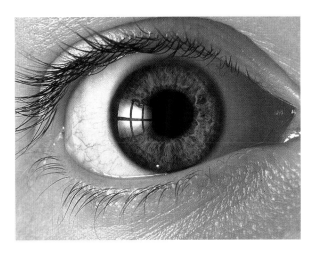

The colour of your eyes is determined by a gene inherited from each of your parents.

over many generations the organism may undergo evolutionary change.

Occasionally, genes mutate - they undergo change and behave differently. This occurs randomly and some genes are more prone to mutations than others. Mutations are the main source of new genes which create variation between individuals. Some mutations are advantageous and the individual is more likely to survive and reproduce to pass the mutated genes onto new generations. Others are harmful and the individual dies. Only a mutation which occurs within a sex cell can be inherited, a mutation affecting a body cell will not. Environmental influences such as background radiation and UV light can increase the rate of mutation. As we will read later, the variation generated by gene mutations is important in plant and animal breeding.

2. The nuts and bolts of genetic engineering

People have been altering the appearance of plants and animals for hundreds of years. Farmers have improved crop plants and animals by selecting those individuals that had the best yield to be parents to the next generation. But selective breeding is a slow and uncertain process. In the case of large animals such as a cow, the female cow may not be ready to breed for a year or two and she only produces one calf at a time. If the calf does not have the desired features, the process would have to be repeated over and over again. It is also hard to predict the result, because a new combination of genes does not necessarily produce a better animal. For example, a cow that produces lots of milk does not always produce calves that give a lot of milk.

Sometimes, a completely new variation may appear amongst the offspring. These sudden changes are due to a mutation. A change has occurred in the DNA, which has resulted in an altered gene. In sheep breeding, for example, a few lambs may be born with particularly short legs. If these lambs are used to breed the subsequent generations, short-legged sheep may result. Sometimes, gardeners have found a different coloured flower among their plants and propagated this plant to produce more. These mutations may be useful, and allow plant and animal breeders to make big improvements, but often they can be harmful and, occasionally, even lethal. The mutant seed may fail to germinate or the animal may be stillborn.

A helping hand

Some new types of crops have been produced by crossing two plant species. For example, oil seed rape only exists because two species

Modern varieties of cereals produce higher yields than the ancestral grasses from which they have been bred.

of cabbage were crossed and a new species produced. This would never have occurred naturally, because the two parent plants grew in different parts of the world. Modern wheat is also a result of human intervention. Through selective breeding, modern wheat has three times as many chromosomes as the ancestral grass from which wheat was developed. The extra chromosomes have given modern wheat increased vigour and higher yields.

Genetic engineering is not that different to selective breeding. But it is a rapid process and is far more precise. The genetic engineer takes a gene that codes for a particular feature from one organism, and inserts it into the DNA of another organism. The result is offspring that carry the new gene and have new abilities.

Genetic breakthrough

The first problem facing the geneticists was to locate particular genes, but being able to remove them from the rest of the DNA was a bigger problem. One of the most important advances in genetic engineering came when scientists discovered an enzyme that could cut DNA at a specific point, a type of molecular "scissors". This meant that it was possible to take out a piece of DNA from one organism using the molecular scissors and insert it into the DNA from another organism. Geneticists now have thousands of different molecular scissors available, each of which can cut DNA at a different place.

This technology is used to create genetically engineered micro-organisms such as bacteria and fungi or to grow cells that can make new products.

One of the largest opportunities of this new technology has been in the fields of human and animal medicine. Many of the substances that are used to treat disease are proteins. Until the arrival of this new technology these proteins had to be extracted from other animals. For example, the protein insulin is used to treat diabetics. Insulin taken from pigs is not identical to human insulin so it can cause side effects in the patient such as an allergic response. By using the new gene technology, the human protein can be manufactured and given to diabetics. The manufacturing process allows large amounts of pure product to be produced at a fraction of the original cost. The purity of the product is important. There is a chance that a product taken from other animals is contaminated with viruses or other foreign substances. A few people have died as a result of receiving human growth hormone contaminated with a virus, and many haemophiliacs have become HIV positive

The selective breeding of cows has produced high-yielding dairy cows that produce 26,000 kg of milk each year.

Engineering human insulin — the genetic way

A technician monitors fermenter units that are used to produce the protein insulin.

1. First, the gene for insulin is located on a human chromosome and removed using a 'cutting' enzyme. The enzyme makes two breaks in the DNA, one on either side of the insulin gene. It cuts the two strands of the DNA in such a way as to leave one strand of the DNA longer than the other. This creates strands with 'sticky' ends.

2. The insulin gene is inserted into a circular strand of bacterial DNA called a plasmid. One enzyme breaks open the plasmid and another joins the sticky ends of the plasmid to those of the human DNA. This is called gene splicing. The result is recombinant DNA, that is DNA composed of DNA from more than one organism.

3. The plasmid is inserted into a bacterial cell which continues to grow and divide as normal. This bacterial cell can now make human insulin.

For commercial production, the bacteria are grown in huge vats and their product, insulin, can be removed easily. This method is cheaper and the product is very pure.

Diabetics using human insulin suffer from fewer side effects compared with the use of insulin extracted from pigs.

as a result of receiving contaminated supplies of factor VIII which is extracted from human blood.

Jurassic genes?

The stars of the film *Jurassic Park* were the dinosaurs. According to the story, they had been recreated from DNA. The scientists had taken dinosaur blood from the bodies of biting insects that had been fossilised in amber. They had removed the dinosaur DNA, repaired it and inserted it into the unfertilised egg of a crocodile and, a few months later, hatched some genetically engineered dinosaurs.

Although we cannot recreate a complete individual, as in the film, it is possible to insert extra genes into the DNA of an animal. The genes may come from another animal, a plant, or even a micro-organism such as a bacterium. An animal that carries foreign DNA in its own DNA is called a transgenic animal. The change in its DNA means that it is different from other animals of the same type — it is a new strain.

Of mice and sheep ... and goats

The organism that has received a new gene has new abilities. It may be able to make a new protein or enzyme, or produce a substance such as an antibiotic. The first experiments were carried out on mice. Scientists injected some DNA into the nucleus of a fertilised egg, and the extra DNA joined to one of the chromosomes to become a permanent part of the mouse's genetic make-up. The altered egg was placed back inside the mother mouse and allowed to develop as normal. The mouse gave birth to a youngster which contained the new genes. One of the first genetically altered mice had a gene which made it grow to a much larger size than normal.

There are sheep with a gene taken from the angora goat, which produces a very high quality wool. Since angora goats are not easy to keep, sheep carrying the angora's wool gene would make it easier to produce large quantities of angora wool.

Animal DNA can be altered so that the animal produces a substance that would normally be difficult, or expensive, to manufacture. For example, a particular transgenic goat carries a human gene. It produces milk that contains a drug. The drug contains a substance which stops human blood from clotting. The milk is collected and the substance extracted and purified. By altering the goat's DNA in

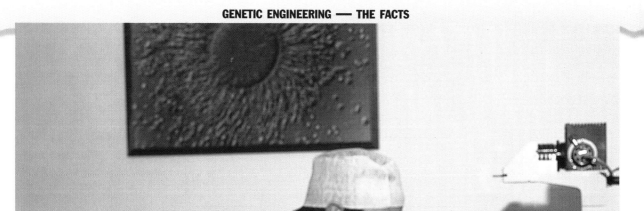

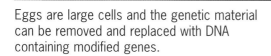
Eggs are large cells and the genetic material can be removed and replaced with DNA containing modified genes.

this way, the animal has become a living 'drug factory' (see also page 62).

At the moment, the only way to produce new transgenic animals is to alter the DNA of normal embryos. This is an expensive procedure, so transgenic animals are very valuable. In the future, however, as genetic technology improves, scientists may be able to recreate exact copies or clones.

> **Am I really alone in feeling profoundly apprehensive about many of the early signals from this brave new world [of genetic engineering] and the confidence, bordering on arrogance, with which it is being promoted?**
>
> HRH The Prince of Wales

Cloning copies

Once a genetically altered organism has been produced, scientists need to be able to produce more of the same without changing the DNA in any way. They need exact copies, or clones. If genetically modified plants or animals were allowed to breed with each other, the new genes could be lost or masked.

Genetically altered bacteria are easy to reproduce because they multiply asexually by dividing into two. The DNA remains the same. Within an hour, one bacterium has multiplied several times over. Plants, however, multiply by sexual reproduction when the pollen from one flower fertilises the egg of another flower. The plants that grow from seed are never identical to either of the parent plants; instead

Genetically modified plants can be grown from a single cell using culture media.

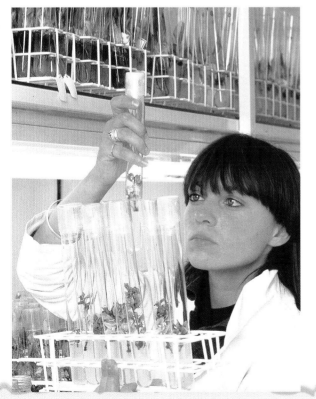

> ## Soon the first human created from a piece of skin will be born. And the world will seem to shudder a little and spin on.
>
> Andrew Marr, *The Independent*, February 1997

they show characteristics of both parents. So even if both parents carry the same genetically modified genes, there is no guarantee that the offspring will inherit these characteristics.

Cloning plants is straightforward. For hundreds of years, gardeners have made exact copies or clones of plants, simply by taking and growing cuttings. A section of stem is cut and placed in the ground. New roots and shoots quickly develop and it grows into a new plant, identical in every way to its parent.

Now, scientists can take just one plant cell and, using growth media, produce an embryo plant. This is given a protective coating and then sown in the ground. Huge numbers of identical plants — clones — can be produced in this way from just one original specimen. Already this technique is used to multiply plants such as orchids that are difficult to reproduce from seed.

Dolly the sheep

Making clones of animals, especially mammals, is more difficult. So the arrival of Dolly, the world's first cloned sheep, was seen as a major step forward. Cells were taken from the donor sheep and grown in the lab. An unfertilised egg was taken from another sheep and the nucleus removed to make sure that there was no genetic material present. A nucleus was taken from one of the cultured cells and inserted into the now empty egg cell. This egg was placed inside a surrogate mother sheep where it developed as normal. Four months later Dolly was born. She is genetically identical to the donor sheep. However, she will never be totally identical because she has been raised in a different environment and has had different experiences. It is a bit like identical twins. They have the same genes, but have their own personalities. News of Dolly has sparked off a great debate about the ethics of this type of research and has raised the possibilities of human clones.

Research into cloning continues and the first cloned cattle were born in 1997 and the first goats in 1999. It is thought likely that within 20 years 85 per cent of British cattle could be cloned from the best quality animals. There are other benefits. There are many rare breeds of

> **The idea that you can bring back a child, that you can bring back your father, it is simply nonsensical. You can make a genetically identical copy, but you cannot get back the person you have lost.**
>
> Dr Wilmut of the Roslin Institute, Scotland (where Dolly was produced)

animals at risk of dying out. Cells could be taken from these animals, frozen and stored for the future. Cloned animals could be produced from these cells. In the future, as genetic technology improves, scientists will be able to produce clones in greater numbers.

IVF (*in vitro* fertilisation) treatment involves the removal of eggs and their fertilisation outside the mother's body. the resulting embryo is placed in the uterus. Currently, researchers are not allowed to engineer either human eggs or sperm or the early cells of an embryo which is to be placed back into the mother.

Dolly – the world's first cloned sheep – attracted much attention when she was first presented to the press.

Human cloning

Imagine being able to recreate a person from DNA taken from their cells. In 1984, an American magazine published an article which investigated the possibility of recreating Elvis Presley from preserved cells taken from his body! Today, this still remains a fantasy, but scientists are making rapid progress in this area of genetic science.

In November 1998, an American research group called American Cell Technology successfully cloned human cells using a technique similar to that used to produce Dolly. An egg was taken from a cow and the DNA removed and replaced with DNA taken from a human leg cell. The new cell was then chemically persuaded to behave like a new embryo and start dividing. The 'embryo' was allowed to develop for 12 days before it was destroyed. This is about the same period that elapses for a natural human embryo to reach the female uterus and implant or bury itself in the uterus lining. This research is part of a project to produce human stem cells. These are so-called 'master cells' which have the ability to develop into any type of cells, such as a blood, skin, brain or liver cell. These cells could produce tissues and organs that would be perfect for transplant operations and for treating patients with diseases such as Parkinson's.

DNA dilemma

DNA technology is not new. It has been developing steadily over the last 25 years, but is only now beginning to affect our daily lives. Some of the principles of the technology are similar to traditional techniques. Plant propagation is cloning, although it is rarely called by that name. The more serious ramifications of the technology, however, are the ways in which it is being applied. For example, new genes can be inserted into plants and animals, and then they can be cloned.

The latest developments in the field of cloning are raising a number of ethical problems. American Cell Technology have made it clear that their research is for medical purposes only and the research will not be used for human reproduction. Opponents say that the development of the technology makes the eventual birth of a human clone inevitable. This, they say, would have profound implications for the nature of family relationships, the law and health.

The dangers of abuse of this technology, whether through accident or design, are many, but so are the potential rewards. This creates a powerful dilemma.

Is it right to alter the genetic make-up of an animal just so it can be used as a living drugs factory? Do we want research into human cloning to continue?

3. The changing face of farming

Rows of GM corn grown as part of a crop trial in Illinois, USA.

Over the last 50 years, the world has witnessed some astounding improvements in agricultural productivity. This has been called a 'green revolution'. In this time, the world's wheat harvest has increased four-fold, and the rice harvest has doubled. But, in order to achieve such high yields, farming has become highly intensive and larger quantities of fertilisers and pesticides have had to be used. More land has been cultivated and natural habitats, such as rainforest and grassland, have been cleared to make way for farmland.

The world now has to come to terms with a 'gene revolution'. Today the area of farmland under GM crops is in excess of 52 million hectares. GM soya and maize make up approximately 80 per cent of this area. The manufacturers of these crops claim that farmers will be able to grow crops that can protect themselves against pests and diseases, grow in more extreme climates, and survive frost or salty soils. We are told that these 'wonder crops' will help feed the world, but will also be kinder to the environment. In this and the following chapters, such claims will be examined.

In Malaysia, a man uses weedkiller on a palm plantation (above) without protective clothing; (right) preparing to spray weedkiller on a golf course in the UK.

Protection against pests

In Europe, our crops are eaten by just a few pests, such as caterpillars and carrot flies. In the tropics, there are many more pests, some of which are incredibly damaging. Locusts, for example, devastate vast areas each year in Africa, consuming a whole crop in just a few hours. Even in a good year, African farmers often lose half their crops to pests or disease.

One way to produce more food is to reduce the number of pests that eat the crops. The traditional method is to use pesticides — chemicals that kill pests such as insects. Many kill insects indiscriminately, destroying useful as well as harmful insects. Others are specific and are designed to kill just one insect species. In addition, many pesticides are poisonous

and are a threat to the health of people, especially the farmers who apply them. In many parts of the world, farmers do not have the correct equipment to make up and apply the pesticides. Often they mix the pesticide into water with their hands. In one district of Andhra Pradesh in India, 500 farmers died of pesticide exposure in 2001 alone.

Some pesticides are designed to break down once they have been in the soil after a few weeks, so that they do not persist in the environment. If a heavy downpour occurs shortly after spraying, the pesticide can be washed off the crops, forcing the farmer to use more. If the pesticide is still active when it enters a watercourse, it can kill aquatic life. Pesticides are generally expensive, and often not very effective. In the southern USA, crops may be sprayed up to eight times a year, yet still one sixth of the crop may be lost to pests.

Tomatoes on trial

Chemical sprays could be avoided if plants could be made to produce a poison to kill certain pests. The bacterium *Bacillus thuringiensis*, which is found in the soil, produces a highly selective poison that is toxic to caterpillars, but generally harmless to other organisms. Geneticists identified the gene that makes the poison, removed it from the bacterial DNA, and inserted it into the DNA of a tomato plant. The altered plant looks just like a normal tomato. To test it, the scientists took some normal and some altered plants and introduced some caterpillars. They found that normal leaves were eaten, but the leaves from the modified plant were avoided. The first stage of the experiment worked — the tomato had the self-protecting gene. But the scientists still had to answer a lot of questions. Were they sure that the toxin made by the plant was exactly the same as that made by the bacterium? The poison must not be changed in any way, otherwise it might affect other organisms. Did it affect useful insects, such as honey bees? The results of the experiments were so encouraging that the gene, known as Bt, was inserted into a number of crop plants.

Chinese scientists have put the Bt gene into cabbage. A major pest of cabbages is the cabbage white butterfly. It lays its eggs on the cabbage leaves and the caterpillars munch their way through the plants. Cabbages protected by Bt contain a poison that kills the caterpillars. This cabbage is not yet available commercially.

Of caterpillars and cotton

Cotton crops can be ravaged by the bollworm, a moth caterpillar. Today, approximately 70 per cent of the US cotton crop is GM cotton. Approximately half are plants with in-built resistance to herbicide and the other half have been given the Bt gene for pest resistance. GM cotton is also grown on a smaller scale in Argentina, Australia, China, Mexico, South Africa, and most recently, India. For many Indian cotton farmers, the arrival of the GM cotton seed isn't a minute too soon. There are nine million hectares of cotton fields (the

Genetically engineered cotton makes up more than one quarter of the US cotton harvest.

world's largest area of cotton) but the average yield in India is only 321 kg per hectare compared with 769 kg per hectare in the US. The farmers have been struggling to find the money to pay for the pesticides, without which the yields are poor. Although the GM cotton seeds cost four times more than conventional seeds, they require 70 per cent fewer pesticides.

Soya savings

Soya is a crop that is grown extensively in the US and Brazil. It is a major source of protein and is used widely in processed food and animal feeds. Approximately one third of the UK's soya comes from Brazil.

Genetically engineered varieties of soya bean have been developed which are unaffected by specific weedkillers containing glyphosate, because they contain a gene from a soil bacterium that is resistant to glyphosate. This means that the farmer can spray the fields to get rid of weeds without affecting the crop, a big advantage. Before the arrival of this soya bean, farmers could only use selective weedkillers, which were expensive and often persisted in the ground for many months. The glyphosate weedkiller is non-selective but it is cheaper and does not persist in the soil. So this new soya bean saves the farmer money (see full discussion on page 34).

The company that developed the glyphosate-resistant soya bean is the same company that manufactures the glyphosate weedkiller, so a farmer buying soya seeds has to buy the weedkiller from the same source. The seeds are more expensive, but the weedkiller is cheaper, and together they give better yields.

The glyphosate-resistant soya bean is just one of several weedkiller-resist-

ant crop plants. Modified sugar beet, oil seed rape and maize are currently undergoing trials, both in the UK and other European countries (see page 49 on field trials).

The salad story

Salad foods do not stay fresh very long and there is a lot of wastage as they spoil on supermarket shelves. If the ripening process could be slowed down, the producers would have more time to get their fruit and vegetables to market and there would be less waste. Tomato growers in the US have achieved just this by means of genetic engineering. One of the first genetically engineered tomatoes to be sold to the public in the US was marketed as the 'flavr savr' tomato. This tomato stayed in top condition for several days longer than other tomatoes. Other modified salad vegetables are in the pipeline, including cucumber that is resistant to disease and celery that stays crisp for longer.

Genetically engineered tomatoes look identical to normal tomatoes, but they may have a longer shelf life or more resistance to disease.

The perfect purée

Scientists first started to study the ripening of the tomato twenty years ago. Their aim then was not to produce a better tomato, but to develop a fruit that could be transported without refrigeration, while retaining its texture and flavour. They also wanted to produce high quality fruit juices and purées that required less processing and fewer additives. They identified an enzyme called pectinase, which helped ripening by breaking down the pectin, which holds the plant cell walls together, allowing the fruit to soften.

By removing a particular gene, cutting a bit off, and then replacing the gene, they were able to stop the enzyme from working. The altered tomato ripened more slowly, allowing shops to have it on sale for a few more days. The tomatoes remained firm, were easy to handle during transport, and there was much less waste. This new tomato is now being used in tomato purée. Purées cannot be too wet, and excess water has to be removed. The new tomatoes contain less water, so less energy is used during the processing; a factor reflected in the reduced cost of the genetically engineered purée when compared to conventional purée. The tomato paste has been approved for sale in the European Union, but not the tomatoes themselves.

> GM has been one of the most important issues for our customers over the past few months and we wanted to make a clear statement... The major concern has been with GM soya protein, so this is where we have concentrated our efforts... We have sourced non-GM soya proteins, oils and lecithins so that all new products being made for Sainsbury's are free from GM soya ingredients.
>
> Dino Adriano, Sainsbury's Group Chief Executive, 1999

Disease-resistant papaya

The papaya ring spot virus is an incurable disease of the papaya, which ruins the fruits and eventually kills the plants. Over the last seven years, the disease has spread across Hawaii, killing thousands of hectares of trees and destroying an $18 million industry. It has also devastated industry in other countries. Now there is a genetically engineered papaya that is resistant to the papaya ring spot virus. The first fruits on commercial farms were harvested in 1999 and went on sale in the US. Hawaii's farmers have planted about 500 hectares in GM papaya, which represents one third of the papaya hectarage in the state. Although the new plants have given Hawaiian farmers a new chance, the debate about benefits versus risks continues. Organic farmers are concerned about ecological risks such as pollen "contamination". There is also the risk that these new plants will cause the virus to mutate into a far more potent virus. However similar risks also exist with conventional crops that are bred to be disease resistant. At the same time, the international backlash against GM crops has begun to hit papayas. There is concern that there may not now be a sufficient market for GM papayas. Up to 40 per cent of the Hawaiian harvest is sold to Japan, where genetically modified papayas have not been approved for sale.

The future of the papaya harvest in Hawaii is dependent on a GM variety that is resistant to ring spot virus.

The self-shearing sheep

Sheep need to be sheared at the beginning of summer every year. The hair of some older breeds of sheep falls off naturally, but commercial sheep have lost this ability. Now, genetic engineers in Australia have managed to produce a protein that can cause the sheep to self-shear. They inject the sheep with a substance that temporarily stops their hair from growing at the hair follicle deep in the skin. After just one day, the hair starts growing again normally, but the halt in growth leaves a natural break in the hair. After four to six weeks, the break appears at the surface of the skin and the fleece can be peeled off. The only drawback is that the farmers have to wrap the sheep in a plastic 'hairnet' to stop the fleece dropping off before it is ready to be collected.

Fighting flies

In summer, sheep are plagued by blowflies. The flies lay their eggs in the sheep's fleece and, when the maggots hatch, they burrow down into the skin and start eating. This leaves nasty sores that can get infected, and the sheep may even die. To prevent blowfly attack, farmers spray their sheep with insect repellent, which contains a number of different chemicals. It has to be applied several times during the summer. There is now a possibility that sheep will be given a gene that will enable them to secrete an insecticide from their skin, providing an in-built year-round protection.

The super-cow

The modern cow is very different from that seen on farms fifty years ago. Traditional methods of breeding have produced a cow with a greatly increased milk yield. Just twenty years ago, the average annual milk yield from a cow was 3000 litres. Today that has almost doubled. But these yields are only obtained if the cow's diet is carefully controlled. The cow has to be given large quantities of expensive food concentrates, rich in fat and protein, in order to produce maximum milk yield. The modern dairy farmer monitors each cow's milk yield and adjusts her diet accordingly. Often the cows spend much of the day in barns, rather than grazing on fields. This way they expend less energy moving around and keeping warm, so that there is more energy to use for milk production. Now technology is offering farmers the opportunity of pushing the milk yield higher still.

Cows produce a substance called bovine somatotrophin, or BST, which is a growth hormone. It is produced throughout the life of the cow, helping dairy cows to produce more milk and beef cattle to lay down more muscle. The cows that produce the most BST produce the most milk and meat.

By injecting their cows with BST, farmers can boost their yields. Originally the hormone was extracted from the brains of dead cattle, but now it is produced in large quantities by genetically engineered bacteria. It is called recombinant bovine somatotrophin or rBST (also known as rBGH or recombinant bovine growth hormone). If dairy cows are given injections of rBST every fourteen days, they produce as much as 12 per cent more milk. In some cases, milk production has increased by 20 per cent. The cows digest their food more efficiently, so the dairy farmer gets more milk for less food and this makes his herd more profitable.

But rBST is not good news for the cows. The cows tend to become sick more often. They suffer udder infections, digestive upsets and lameness, and are prone to sores and cuts which do not heal quickly. As a result, the cows have to be fed more antibiotics to maintain their fitness.

There are also health implications. Trace amounts of BST are naturally present in milk and meat. So it is not surprising that milk from BST-treated cows can contain traces of rBST. This means that the whole range of dairy products, from milk and cheese to yoghurts and baby foods, may contain the hormone, and possibly traces of the antibiotics. So far, tests have proved that these levels of BST do not harm human health. But the long-term effects are not known. rBST milk also contains high levels of protein called Insulin-like-Growth Factor One or IGF-1. This is a chemical that has been linked to cancer, especially breast and prostate cancers. It is also the factor that causes the increased illness in the cows.

In 1994, the US Food and Drug Administration approved the use of the hormone. US milk products containing rBST do not have to be labelled as such. In a test case, one dairy farmer labelled his milk as BST-free and was sued in court by the manufacturer of rBST, Monsanto. The court upheld the Monsanto argument that the label implied that rBST-containing milk was harmful.

The milk is banned in Australia, New Zealand, Japan and in the European Union. The EU has accepted that milk from treated cows represents a risk to human health as well as raising animal welfare issues. There is currently a moratorium on the marketing and use of the product in the European Union.

Injecting dairy cows with BST can increase the milk yield by as much as 20 per cent.

The European Union decision has been upheld by the United Nations Food Safety Agency, which represents 101 nations world-wide. On 18 August 1999, the agency ruled unexpectedly in favour of the European moratorium on the rBST milk. This means that the US has had to drop its threat of challenging the European moratorium at the World Trade Organisation. This ruling is a milestone in that it is the first major ruling against genetically modified foods on scientific grounds.

Do we want GM crops and animals?

If one thing is certain, it is that the new varieties of GM crops and animals have the potential to transform farming methods. Over the years, untold damage has been done to the environment by the wholesale application of agro-chemicals. It is not appealing to think that an orange may be sprayed as many as fifteen times before it is harvested and then coated in wax to give it an attractive shine. Apples can be sprayed as many as forty times with a huge range of chemicals. The end result is that many of our foods contain pesticide residues, so it's not surprising that the UK government advises consumers to wash or peel all fruit before eating. Even small amounts of pesticide can affect health and, in the long term, lead to cancers. Some studies have linked breast cancers with the use of lindane, a pesticide that is used on seeds, apples, oil seed rape, sugar beet, wheat and maize.

Discarded pesticide containers at a landfill site in Australia. Today's farmers can choose from a huge range of pesticides but the effect of some of these chemicals on human health and on the environment is not clearly understood.

The new, pest-resistant GM crops require less pesticide and weedkiller application. If yields also increased, then the pressure to farm more land would be reduced. Both the environment and wildlife could benefit. But there is still much uncertainty. The long-term effects of new GM crops are not yet known.

Some of the genetic modifications to animals could actually improve animal welfare. Anyone who has seen a sheep suffering with fly strike, for example, would say that a sheep with natural fly repellents could not come too soon. But there seem to be few benefits of rBST, especially in terms of cattle welfare.

Milk consumption in Europe is falling and there is considerable over-production. This has led to surplus milk powder and butter mountains.

Tough milk quotas are in place and many smaller dairy farms have been forced out of business. A similar trend is seen in the US, where experts are predicting a twenty-five per cent fall in the numbers of dairy cows.

We must ask whether the benefit of cheap milk is so great that we are happy for the health of cows to suffer?

All the crop plants and domesticated animals in the world are the result of thousands of years of deliberate human manipulation. Is the genetic engineering of animals and plants any different?

> GM crops are the same as non-GM crops except for one or two genes out of 50,000-70,000 genes already present in nature. For this reason, there is no justification for categorising them in the same way as highly active drugs.
>
> Clive Rainbird, AgrEvo (a leading company involved with plant health, biotechnology and environmental health) 1999

GE and the food story

We would like to think that most of the food we eat is 'natural and healthy'. But much of our food contains chemical additives, including artificial colouring, preservatives and stabilisers added to food to improve its appearance or flavour, or to keep it fresh for longer. Fresh fruit and vegetables may have been sprayed with pesticides to prevent pests from spoiling their appearance, and a high proportion of processed, ready-made foods already contain genetically engineered maize and soya. However, the levels of any of these substances in foods are strictly monitored and controlled.

There are two different types of GM foods — GM whole foods, such as tomato, papaya and salmon, and processed foods that contain small amounts of products from GM plants. In the US, there is a wide variety of GM foods on sale, including apples, asparagus, barley, beetroot, carrots, cauliflower, grapes, kiwi, lettuce, maize, melons, papaya, peanuts, peppers, potatoes, strawberries, rice, salmon, soya, sugarcane, tomatoes and wheat. Not all of these foods may be sold in the European Union, as they have not yet completed the necessary approval process. So far, the European Union has approved GM maize and soya, and GM tomato for use in processed foods.

The small selection of GM foods approved for sale in the European Union have received a lot of publicity. Emotive words such as 'Franken-foods' (after the fictional character Baron Frankenstein, who created a monster) have been used in the press. So, is there a difference between genetically engineered foods and so called 'normal foods'? And what are the benefits?

In the future, we could be offered a whole range of 'health' foods such as
• tomatoes with increased vitamin content
• non-allergenic peanuts
• potatoes with higher starch content which will absorb less oil in cooking
• wheat with increased levels of folic acid to prevent spina bifida
• wheat with increased fibre to reduce the risk of colon cancer
• tomatoes that can ripen on the vine for better taste but yet have a longer shelf life.

- **Soya beans**: Soya is used in as much as sixty per cent of processed foods, including margarine, smoked herring, doughnuts, cakes, bread and biscuits, meat, tinned soups, pasta sauce, baby food and diet foods. It is also added to food as a binding agent, stabiliser and emulsifier. (Soya oil and rape seed oil may be labelled as 'vegetable fats' or 'hydrogenated vegetable fat'.) GM soya is already widely used and is approved for sale in the European Union and the US.

- **Maize**: Maize is used in up to half of today's processed foods as well as bread, cereals, and dairy products. Maize is also a main ingredient of animal feed. GM maize is approved for sale in the European Union and the US.

- **Oil seed rape**: Oil from rape seed is widely used in vegetable oil, margarine, and tinned and processed foods. GM rape is approved for sale in the US and is currently undergoing field trials in the UK and other countries of the European Union.

- **Sugar beet**: Sugar comes from sugar beet and sugar cane, both of which have GM varieties under trial in the European Union. As well as refined sugar, GM sugar could be used in processed foods such as cakes and biscuits.

- **Potatoes**: The new low-water potato absorbs less fat when fried and could be used in low fat crisps and chips. This potato is currently undergoing field trials in the US.

- **Tomatoes**: Tomatoes such as the non-squashy 'Flavr Savr' ripen slowly and have a long shelf life. Genetically altered tomato may be used in purée, sauces and soups. Currently, in the UK GM tomato may be used in purées and processed foods but the tomatoes may not be eaten whole.

- **Milk**: Farmers may be allowed to inject dairy cows with rBST so they produce more milk. Trace amounts of the hormone appear in the milk. This milk is on sale in the US but not in the European Union.

- **Cheese**: Cheeses labelled as vegetarian may contain chymosin derived from GM yeast. Since the chymosin is a derivative, the cheese does not have to be labelled as containing GM ingredients.

- **Selection of fruits including papaya/strawberries/melons/apples**: A wide range of fruits with genes for pest and frost resistance may appear on supermarket shelves. Many of these fruits are already approved for use in the US.

- **Peanuts**: Nuts can set off potentially fatal allergic reactions in some people. GM nuts under development would avoid this problem.

Food of the future
Some of the foods in this photograph may already contain GM ingredients. In the future, all all of them could contain genetically engineered products.

Trouble with soya beans

The public's awareness of GM foods dates back to the arrival of the first GM soya beans in Europe. The first harvest of genetically altered soya beans took place in 1996. Soya is a remarkably useful product. It is high in protein and natural fat and is a good binding agent. Soy beans are processed into soy meal and soy oil. Most soy meal is used to make high-protein animal feed and the rest is used in foods for human consumption. Today, soya can be found in about sixty per cent of processed foods (see pages 32 and 90). Soya oil can be processed further to produce products such as lecithin which is added to foods as a stabiliser and emulsifier. (Lecithin is sometimes labelled as E322.)

In the US, GM soya makes up more than 75 per cent of the total US crop, that's about fifty-five million tonnes of GM soya. Once harvested, the genetically engineered beans are mixed with normal beans. The beans look the same, so there is no way of telling them apart. Together, they go to the food processors and end up in our food. Many people around the world are very annoyed that we do not know that we are eating genetically engineered food, and do not have the option of choosing. They don't necessarily mind that the beans are being grown, but they do want to decide for themselves whether or not to eat them. In the US, both soya bean farmers and the company that produces the plants are being challenged by an increasingly active campaign. Currently the UK imports all its soya, so has little control over the growing of GM soya. However, there are new non-GM varieties which could be grown in southern England, so some farmers are looking into growing this crop.

European consumers are putting the soya bean producers under pressure, forcing them to devise ways of separating and labelling the engineered soya. DNA tests, which detect

Soy bean is a useful crop and is widely grown, especially in North America and Brazil.

small amounts of genetically engineered soya, can be used to check that the beans have been properly separated. It is likely that the producers will charge more if they have to separate out their GM soya beans. But there is much disagreement about just how much this will cost. So what are the likely costs? Already, the soya producers separate different types of beans. They separate out the beans destined for the Japanese tofu market as well as beans with a high protein content. There is a surcharge of between six and fifteen per cent on top of the basic soya costs for this service. As separation becomes more widespread the costs could come down. But many of the GM companies are claiming that separation costs are far higher, even as much as 150 per cent of the basic cost of soya, and this will push up the price of food. Whether this is scare tactics or reality is unclear. At the moment, there is a battle between the food buyers who need to supply GM-free soya to their consumers and the US soya growers who claim it is impossible to separate the beans. The problem may solve itself to a certain extent as crop trials have revealed that this particular strain of GM soya does not grow as well as normal soya in hot and dry conditions. This will restrict the planting of the crop, at least in the short term.

Prize potatoes — but are they vegetables?

A potato that is resistant to frost would be a big breakthrough. It would mean that potatoes could be grown more widely, and over a longer season. The traditional way of producing new, improved varieties of potatoes by crossing and selecting was not producing results. Then, genetic engineering discovered a way forward. The flounder, a type of flatfish, lives in icy cold waters and has a gene that makes special antifreeze proteins to protect its cells and prevent them from freezing. By inserting this gene into the DNA of a potato, scientists could produce a frost-resistant vegetable. This would mean that the potato would contain an animal gene. So is it still a vegetable? Will vegetarians be prepared to eat it? Much of the DNA in animals and plants is virtually the same, so does the transfer of a small length of animal DNA into a plant make any difference?

Other types of GM potatoes are being developed. Soon, consumers in the US may be able to buy a quick-fry potato. It has been engineered to have a low-water content, which means that it will take less time to cook crisps and chips. At present, it is being considered by food safety committees in the US.

A potato (above) that is resistant to frost would be a big breakthrough; a gene from the flounder (right) can protect potatoes against frost... but is this potato still a vegetable?

Cheese — suitable for vegetarians

Cheese manufacture has used the same basic process for thousands of years. Milk is allowed to become sour, then mixed with a substance called rennet, which causes the protein to clot and become solid. The solids, or curds, are separated from the fluid whey, pressed into shape, and allowed to mature. Rennet is a mixture of substances, including an enzyme called chymosin. Rennet is obtained from the stomach lining of young calves, which is why some vegetarians do not eat cheese made the traditional way. Genetic engineering has changed this situation. The gene to make chymosin was inserted in yeast. Now engineered yeast is used to make large quantities of pure chymosin at very low cost. Although the gene in the yeast originally came from an animal, cheeses made with chymosin have been approved by the Vegetarian Society in the UK. After some debate, it decided to approve the cheeses because young animals no longer had to be slaughtered. Cheeses containing the genetically engineered chymosin are clearly marked with the vegetarian symbol — the letter V. Today, genetically engineered chymosin makes up more than half the world's supply of rennet, but GM food scares have forced cheese manufacturers to look for non-GM sources of chymosin. They have found a yeast that produces a rennet-like protein that can be used in cheese-making.

What risk of an allergic reaction?

People who suffer from a nut allergy can die within minutes of eating a food containing nuts, unless help is immediately available. But what about the genes from a nut in another food? Already a GM soya bean containing a gene taken from the Brazil nut was abandoned before it went on sale because of fears that it might cause allergic reactions in people sensitive to nuts. In contrast, a new GM nut has had the gene that produces the allergic response removed. Many people are allergic to rice. A new rice that does not produce an allergic response has been developed by inactivating the gene that causes the allergy.

In 2000, the risks of new allergies from GM foods surfaced when a few people reported an allergic reaction after eating taco shells. The taco shells were found to have been made from corn that had been contaminated by a new GM variety called Starlink corn. A protein called Cry9C had been inserted into the corn to give it protection against a corn

Many cheese manufacturers are seeking sources of non-GM rennet to replace the chymosin which is made by GM yeasts.

People who eat rice diets often suffer from a lack of iron. This causes anaemia, a medical condition in which a person has a low red blood cell count and tires easily. Now there is a new variety of GM rice which is rich in iron. This rice has three times the normal level of iron found in rice, which means that a person eating a portion of rice would get up to half their daily iron allowance. However, this new variety of rice will have to undergo tests to make sure that it is safe to eat.

borer. The corn had been approved for livestock consumption only. Following this incident more than 300 food products had to be withdrawn from sale and the variety is no longer sold to farmers. Experts believe that it will take at least four years before it will be safe to say that the protein has been removed from the food chain.

Is it safe to eat?

Most countries have laws that require foods containing genetically engineered products to be reviewed and tested. Before any genetically modified food or food ingredient can be sold in the European Union it has to be

Countries such as Britain and Austria have argued against the approval of some GM foods, but they have been over-ruled by the majority of other members. However, in May 1999, the European Union rejected an application for a GM crop for the first time (see below).

Testing times

So, what are the tests and are they really rigorous? In the pharmaceutical industry, new drugs undergo up to fifteen years of clinical trials. Even then, as many as three per cent of new drugs are later withdrawn from sale due to unforeseen side effects. None of the GM foods on sale in the UK has undergone testing that could be considered as rigorous. No long-term trials have ever been done on GM foods, nor are any planned. The GM soya, for example, was tested on rats for just ten weeks. The food tests compare the characteristics of the new GM product with those of a non-GM equivalent. If the products are found to be similar, then the GM product requires no further testing on the assumption that it is no more dangerous that the non-GM equivalent. This is based on a form of risk assessment called substantial equivalence. The foods may be considered 'substantially equivalent', but this form of testing overlooks the possibility that there may be a different protein, which could interact with the existing constituents of the food in a new and unexpected manner.

Genetic markers

There may be some problems with some of the new GM products awaiting approval. One such product is a new type of maize. Maize is

More consumers are demanding that the testing procedures for genetically modified foods are tightened up.

assessed by specialist scientific committees in member countries, for example, the UK's Advisory Committee on Novel Foods and Processes. If any of these committees have objections based on scientific grounds, the product is rejected and referred to the European Commission Standing Committee for Foodstuffs, where it is assessed again. In order to pass for clearance on to the market the Committee must vote by a majority in its favour. In general, companies wishing to market their products in the EU usually only require the permission of one member country. The findings of that country's committees are passed on to the other members and governments, who then decide whether they wish to challenge the findings. There have been a number of disagreements between countries.

an important food ingredient found in half the processed foods in the UK, including bread, cereals, dairy products, and animal feeds. Maize plants are attacked by a tiny pest called the corn borer mite, which chews through the stalks. A new type of genetically engineered maize has been developed to be resistant to the mite. But a marker gene was also added to the maize.

Marker genes are used because they allow the geneticist to see if the genetic engineering has worked. Often, the marker gene is one that makes the organism resistant to the effects of a particular antibiotic. The marker gene in the GM maize gives resistance to ampicillin, a widely used antibiotic. Scientists are worried that, when food containing this gene is eaten, the gene will come into contact with bacteria living in the human gut. There is a very small chance that the gene could pass from the food into the bacteria, making them resistant to the antibiotic.

The companies producing the maize claim that there is no evidence that a gene could transfer in this way, but opponents say, there is always a first time. Furthermore, nobody is quite sure what will happen if we eat large amounts of foods which contain this gene. The latest research shows that foreign DNA lingers for much longer in the gut than previously known. Tests using an artificial gut showed that DNA remains for several minutes in the large intestine and this would be long enough for the DNA associated with ampicillin resistance to become incorporated into bacteria living in the gut, creating antibiotic-resistant strains of gut bacteria.

Some forward-thinking companies have already decided that it would be wise to use other marker genes and avoid this problem. Companies that use these marker genes are hoping to remove the gene before they market any products. However, Ciba-Geigy failed to get its maize with pest- and weedkiller resistance approved for sale in the European

Union because it still contained the ampicillin resistance gene. The maize had initially been approved by France, but it was voted down by other members. This was the first time the European Union had blocked the approval of a genetically engineered crop. However, the maize was approved for sale in Canada and the US. There are a number of other genes that can be used as marker genes. Most biotechnology companies are now removing the controversial marker genes before they submit their products for approval.

The WHO has concluded that the risks of the gene for antibiotic resistance being transferred across the gut are negligible. However, as a precautionary measure, the International Regulatory Authority has recommended that different marker systems are developed. It is also important to consider other sources of antibiotic resistance in the environment. The risk from GM crops that carry antibiotic-resistant genes fades into insignificance, when compared to the overuse of antibiotics world-wide by doctors and livestock farmers.

> **The (US) government isn't listening to growing worries among American consumers. It is too close to the big biotechnology companies who stand to gain billions of dollars from their GM varieties. GM food is not properly labelled in this country and that is robbing consumers of choice.**
>
> Paul Krautmann, organic farmer in USA, 1999

Label laws

In 1992, the US Food and Drug Administration announced that genetically engineered foods would not be treated differently to natural foods. Therefore, the new foods did not require a label stating that they have been genetically engineered. The situation is very different in the European Union. Legally, food-stuffs must be labelled when detectable levels of DNA and/or protein derived from genetic modification are present. Food producers and retailers are obliged to include the phrase 'produced from genetically modified soybean' or 'produced from genetically modified maize' as appropriate on the label. From 21 September 1999, all restaurants and caterers were legally obliged to identify, on their menus, any of their foods containing GM soya or maize.

Most supermarket and restaurant chains have gone to some lengths to remove all GM ingredients from their own brand foods. Animal feed contains a lot of maize, which could contain GM maize grown in North America. So, in the latest moves, some supermarkets are now selling meat from animals that have not been fed on GM animal feed. However, when some foods are processed or refined the DNA is broken down or removed and it becomes impossible to test whether that food ingredient came from a GM source or another source. For example, lecithin from a GM soya plant is chemically indistinguishable from lecithin from a non-GM soya bean. It is used in processed foods as a stabiliser and identified on a food label as E22. Moreover, the chymosin used to make vegetarian cheese is a product of GM yeast and the products of a GM organism are exempt from the labelling legislation. This situation is currently being reviewed at European Union level.

European MEPs have just approved plans to ensure that there is clear labelling of all food derived from GM crops. The labels will apply

> There are reasons, beyond safety or nutrition, for a consumer to want labeling of (GM) food ... including religious, ethical, right-to-know, or simple preference reasons.
>
> *Animal Biotechnology: Science-Based Concerns,* US National Academy of Sciences, 2002

The arrival of GM-containing foods in UK shops resulted in demonstrations and petitions to get the foods removed from the shelves.

to foods which contain more than 0.5 per cent of GM material.

Going organic

Worldwide, the organic food market is booming, with a 15 to 30 per cent growth rate in Europe, Japan and the US over the last five years. By 2010 the market is estimated to rise to £32 billion in Europe, £30 billion in the US and £7 billion in Japan.

At first most of the organic foods on sale were fresh produce such as fruits, vegetables, meat and milk that could be obtained locally. As consumer demand has grown, suppliers have had to look further afield for their supplies, for example importing vegetables out of season. Now there is a demand for more processed organic foods and ready-to-eat meals, so food manufacturers are having to source

Organic vegetable 'box' schemes are becoming increasingly popular. Here, organic vegetables are being sorted and boxed at a local distribution centre.

organic ingredients such as flavourings, essential oils, fruit juices, dried fruits, herbs and spices etc. Often these have to be imported as they are not produced locally.

Genetic guinea pigs?

The public's reaction to GM foods has been highly critical, at least according to the media. Food in Europe has suffered a number of setbacks: first the BSE crisis in the UK during the 1990s, which hit the beef market, and then the dioxin scare in Belgium caused by contaminated animal food. Europeans seem to be increasingly sceptical of their governments' ability to make food safe.

Clear, unambiguous labelling would at least help consumers to make informed purchase choices. They may decide that any potential risk is small and buy the food, or decide to avoid it. Either way, they need to have the information to hand in order to make a choice. For people living in the UK it is relatively easy to avoid GM foods. As a result of public pressure, major supermarket chains are removing as many GM products from their foods as possible. It is probably more difficult to buy a food containing a GM product than it is to avoid it!

However, the legislation only covers foods that contain food derived from a GM organism such as maize, soya and tomatoes. It does not cover all the derivatives of the GM organisms such as chymosin in cheese, starch and lecithin in processed foods.

GM critics point out that these foods have only been around for a few years. The long-term effects of eating GM foods have never been tested. Are we being used as guinea pigs in a global experiment? Or will we reap the benefits?

4. Letting the gene out of the bag — and into the environment

A regular news feature during recent summers has been protestors destroying field trials of GM crops. They took this action because they were concerned that too little was known about the risk to the environment. Many other groups called for a five-year moratorium on field trials to give more time to carry out basic research in the laboratory and greenhouse.

So is there a risk? It is important to remember that genetically engineered organisms are living things, and so are much less predictable, for now, than artificial materials and chemicals. They can reproduce, move, and even mutate. Developments in genetic engineering take place in carefully controlled laboratory conditions. However, once a new or modified organism has been developed, it is likely to be grown outside. Once released into the environment, it cannot be recalled. In many cases, it is impossible to predict the results of contact with other organisms. For example, the organism could change or interbreed with others, creating new species. It is these risks that current research is designed to assess.

The pros and cons of GM crops also need to be considered in relation to the damage done to the environment by

> It was probably a bad PR move to have used antibiotic-resistant genes in plants, but it was no more than that. Certainly such crops pose little danger compared to the antibiotics that are dumped on us by farmers and doctors.
>
> Sir Robert May, Government Chief Scientist, talking to the *Observer*, May 1999

A sign put up by protesters on a fence surrounding a GM-crop field trial.

WARNING

BIOHAZARD

GM CROPS AND POLLEN IN THIS AREA

modern intensive farming methods. Hedges are removed, meadows ploughed up and chemicals sprayed. GM may offer farmers the chance to farm in a more environmentally friendly way, while still maintaining crop yield.

Farmers often use weedkillers that persist in the ground for several weeks, even months, to kill any weeds and stop new ones from germinating. These weedkillers are designed to kill one particular group of weeds — broad-leafed weedkillers kill weeds with broad leaves, leaving narrow-leafed cereal crops such as wheat and maize unharmed. Though the crops are tolerant of the weedkiller, they often experience a setback in growth rate. However, the most environmentally friendly weedkillers are the contact ones, which kill plants, but do not persist in the soil. They are based on a chemical called glyphosate. Glyphosate is commonly found in weedkillers used by gardeners to clear weeds from paths but because glyphosate-based weedkillers are not selective the farmers cannot use them as they would kill the crops.

The new GM crops are different to the normal crops in that they can be sprayed with glyphosate and remain unaffected. These crops offer some environmental benefits. The traditional method for crop cultivation is to turn the soil just before seeding. A persistent soil-based weedkiller, such as atrazine, is used to kill off any weeds that germinate. This chemical has an adverse effect on the worms and other animals in the soil. Further applications of the weedkiller may be sprayed later in the season. When GM crops are sown, they are drilled straight into undisturbed soil. This reduces water loss from the soil, stopping it from drying out and blowing away. The farmers don't have to spray as soon as weeds appear — the spraying can be left in the knowledge that one spraying will kill all the weeds. Until that time, insects and birds can feed on the flowers and seeds of the weeds. After spraying, the dead weeds form a mulch on the ground, reducing water loss from the soil and preventing soil erosion — an important feature in dry areas and on sandy soils. The mulch acts to stop more weeds germinating, so it is a useful weed suppressant.

> **They (British farmers) have no choice when it comes to GM crops. The truth is that if something is more effective, such as pesticide-resistant GM cotton, and farmers want to use it because they want to spray less pesticide, let's do it... (The use of GM cotton) is down to an economic calculation — whether farmers want to pay a little more for the seed and less for the pesticide. Given my knowledge of pesticides, I would rather pay more for the seed.**
>
> Dr James Watson talking about British agriculture (Nobel prize winner for his work with Francis Crick on DNA)

Bt alert

The pest-resistant crops have other advantages. The corn borer larvae that attack maize plants and the boll worm larvae that infest cotton, tunnel into the plants. Traditional sprays do not reach the larvae. In the GM plants containing the Bt gene (see page 24), the larvae are poisoned when they eat the plants. But some scientists are concerned about the use of the Bt gene. The larvae are not actually killed by the toxin, just stopped from eating the plant. There is a chance that some of the larvae will become resistant to the toxin. There is more likelihood of this happening if these GM plants are planted across a wider area. Organic farmers are also upset, because they use a Bt powder, which they spray over their crops. Although it is difficult to use, they have no alternative method. Scientists believe that resistance to Bt could be widespread within a few years. If the larvae become resistant to the toxin, organic farmers' crops will also be affected.

Benefits for birds?

After five years of growing GM cotton, soya and maize, some US farmers are reporting an upsurge in hawks, owls and other birds on their land. This has been linked to the recovery of insect life on farms which were previously sprayed repeatedly and heavily to protect crops. Insect-eating birds such as pheasant and quail are increasing and these are eaten by predators, such as the hawks and owls. One Illinois farmer with 230 hectares planted with GM maize and soya reports seeing owls and red-tailed hawks on his farm for the first time in years. In the traditional fields where he still uses pesticides, he finds dead birds that eat the grubs and insects. Organic farmers in the region also report seeing more bird and insect life. However, conservationists argue that the change in bird life could be due to changes in farm practice, such as measures to counter soil erosion. Unfortunately, there are no scientific

The UK government has undertaken to restore declining species such as the corn bunting. Will the spread of GM crops help or hinder this task?

studies to back up any of these observations.

It seems that carefully managed GM crops may offer some environmental benefits. However, UK conservation organisations are concerned that the over-effective control of weeds or pests could result in less food or habitat for insects and the birds that depend on them. As many as twenty different kinds of weeds may grow around a field, providing food for a huge range of insects and birds. Although the farmers use fewer weedkillers on GM crops, they are able to apply a single large dose, which leads to more effective weed control. If farmers start controlling weeds more effectively, this important food source may be lost to wildlife. The UK government has undertaken to restore declining species such as the skylark and corn bunting, but this task could be made more difficult by changes in farm practice linked to GM crops.

The threat to wildlife

The introduction of GM crops into the countryside could threaten native wildlife. Genetically engineered crops such as the new soya bean, maize and cotton have only been studied in a few field tests. Now they are grown extensively across the US. The greater the area over which the crops are grown, the greater the risk. There are many as yet unanswered questions about these plants. Here are just a few:

• Will the plants threaten other animals and plants?
• Will the genes spread into other ecosystems?
• Will the genes cross over to wild relatives or traditional strains?
• Will the plants change in the long term due to their resistance to toxic substances?

There is, as yet, no evidence one way or the other regarding these fears.

The survival of the species

Some scientists think that genetically engineered plants and animals will threaten the survival of other species, and reduce biodiversity (the number of different plant and animal species). The genetically engineered plants may be more resistant to disease or pests, and hence they may grow stronger and be more successful than other plants. If they are successful, genetically engineered plants will soon be grown all round the world. The native soya bean comes from Australia and the Pacific islands. When the new modified soya bean is grown in these regions, there is a risk that the new genes will cross to the wild species. The wild population of the bean would be contaminated, which could affect local habitats and the wildlife species that grow there.

Members of the cabbage family breed easily with wild relatives. Oil seed rape was produced by crossing two varieties of cabbage. This may mean that genetically engineered oil seed rape will breed with related plants, and the new gene for resistance to weed killer could spread into the wild population. Some scientists predict that, within just one year, a large percentage of weeds growing near the crop would have acquired this gene. The result could be super-weeds which would be impossible to kill using glyphosate-based weedkillers.

Mexico is the home of hundreds of varieties of maize which are allowed to cross-breed to produce the best crops for extreme conditions. To preserve this valuable gene bank, the Mexican government banned the planting of GM crops in 1998. However, the government has now confirmed that despite this ban, there is massive contamination of the maize. A survey carried out in 2001 dis-

Nothing can stop the wind and insects from carrying pollen from one plant over great distances and cross-pollinating other plants. But does the possibility of cross-pollination from a GM crop pose a real threat?

covered evidence of contamination at the majority of the test sites, even those in the most remote regions of the country. It appears that maize imported into Mexico from the US for the production of tortillas may have been used as seed by farmers who were unaware that some of it originated from GM crops. The worst contamination was found near the main roads, along which maize is sold to villagers. The contaminated seeds were identified by the presence of the cauliflower mosaic virus, which is used widely in GM crops to "switch on" insecticides which have been inserted within them.

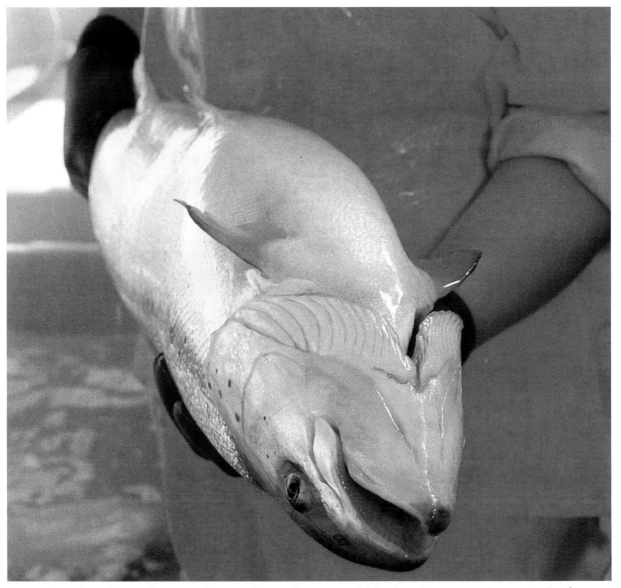

Researchers have inserted a copy of a growth gene into eggs of Atlantic salmon to produce a strain of genetically engineered salmon that has the potential to grow at four times the rate of farmed salmon.

Animal invasion

Often the introduction of a new animal into an environment can result in native species being replaced. Sometimes, the introduced species is so successful that it undergoes a population explosion and may even be classed as a pest. For example, the rabbit was introduced to Australia where it is now a pest. The introduction of the Nile perch to Lake Victoria has led to the extinction of several native species of fish and the disruption of the lake's ecosystem. Among the genetically modified animals under development is a GM salmon. The GM Atlantic salmon can grow up to six times faster than normal, although the final size is the same. It means that these fish can be brought to market size in as little as a year, improving the profitability of fish farming. However, many people are concerned that the GM salmon could escape from open water pens and breed with native salmon. The new genes would then spread into the wild population. Also, the GM salmon have larger appetites than the wild salmon so could disrupt the local ecosystem. The escape of GM salmon from open water pens is inevitable. As many as 20 per cent of salmon on such farms escape during storms and in some parts of Norway escaped salmon outnumber wild salmon by five to one. The companies producing the GM salmon claim that they will only be selling sterile females so there is no chance of the fish breeding with the wild salmon. However the process of producing these sterile females is not always 100 per cent reliable and it is possible that a few fertile females could slip through. The answer may be to restrict these fish to closed systems on land. Land-based systems are more expensive to build but have definite environmental advantages

Pollen surprise in field trials

Pollen from flowers can spread over large distances, carried by the wind or by insects such as bees. Field trials in the UK require the GM crops to be surrounded by a barrier crop. For example, guidelines for oil seed rape field trials require there to be a 6m barrier of non-GM oil seed rape

> **These trials are a farce. They will produce little or no useful scientific evidence on the environmental effects of GM crops. They are an environmental hazard in themselves.**
>
> Friends of the Earth Food Campaigner Adrian Bebb, talking about the GM farm scale field trials in Britain 1999

> **We do realise there are uncertainties, particularly about the effect of genetic modification on biodiversity, on wildlife in the countryside... That is exactly why we have set up the farm scale evaluations, a four-year programme to find out the facts and the truth.**
>
> Michael Meacher, Environment Minister, speaking on the *Today* programme, BBC Radio 4, 1999

around the GM oil seed rape plants to reduce the likelihood of cross-pollination with other crops. At the end of the trial, all plants in a 50m zone around the trial have to be removed. In addition, the trial GM oil

Bees could be responsible for carrying GM pollen from GM plants to non-GM plants.

seed rape must be grown at least 200m from the nearest non-GM oil seed rape crop.

However, the pollen blown from fields of GM oil seed rape remains fertile over greater distances than expected. Oil seed rape is a plant that readily cross-pollinates with other plants, so some spread of the resistance to unmodified crops grown close by was expected. Even so, scientists investigating the spread of pollen found surprising results. It was discovered that oil seed rape plants growing as far as 400m from the test plants produced seven per cent of seed with herbicide resistance. This means they had to have been pollinated by GM pollen. At 100m as many as one quarter of the seeds were resistant. The UK government is still recommending a 200m buffer zone between GM and non-GM oil seed rape, which is twenty-five times lower than the 5 km limit recommended by the European Commission. Even with a 5 km buffer zone, the Commission believes that as much as 0.3 per cent of oil seed rape could

The (UK) Government is in a state of chaos and confusion over GM buffer zones.
Peter Melchett, Policy Director of the
Soil Association 2002

be contaminated. In the US there is a 400m buffer zone and genetic contamination is commonplace.

The government in the UK has been very open about the field trials, with the sites being advertised in the local press.

The crop destruction during the summer of 1999 raised the public's awareness of the GM field trials, but it prevented researchers from carrying out essential research into the potential risks. As a result of public pressure, the government has agreed that there will be no commercial planting of GM crops in the UK until spring 2003 at the earliest. The field trials will continue to allow researchers to obtain the information they require. The trials will be limited to spring and autumn planted GM oilseed rape, maize and sugar beet. There will be approximately 20-25 fields per crop. This works out at 200 hectares spread over the country. There will be a 'cordon sanitaire' around the fields and the crops will be destroyed after harvest.

The UK is not the only country in which GM crop trials are being carried out. These trials are being carried out around the world. As regulations concerning field trials are tightened in Europe, the biotech companies are moving to the developing world to complete their trials. But of course the same potential risks exist to the indigenous plants and animals of the developing world.

Initial research indicated that GM crops, especially GM maize, could adversely effect the monarch butterflies which fly from winter roosting sites in Mexico and California to spend the summer in central and northern states of the USA. However, a number of research groups have investigated this further and found that if there is any effect it is very small. The butterflies face a greater threat from destruction of the trees in which they spend winter (see picture on page 52).

Organic concerns

Organic farmers are concerned about the GM crops. In order to gain approval by the Soil Association and other organisations, organic food is not allowed to contain any foreign DNA. If GM crops are grown close to organic crops there is potential for cross-pollination, causing

Organic farming is far more labour intensive since pesticides and weedkillers are not used. The close proximity of a GM crop could threaten the livelihood of an organic farmer.

the organic crop to become contaminated. This would reduce the value of the organic crop. For example, in Canada, a number of organic farmers have been unable to sell their corn as organic because it has been con-taminated by GM crops grown on neighbouring farms. Foods that claim to be GM-free can be tested to prove that they do not contain any foreign DNA. In 2000, the EU Commission ordered a study of the co-exis-tence of GM and non-GM crops. When the report was completed in 2002, the commission decid-ed not to make the results of the study public, but the report was leaked to Greenpeace. The report makes it clear that it would be economically difficult, if not impossible, for GM and non-GM oilseed rape to co-exist without genetic contamination.

Some people think that GM maize will threaten the survival of the monarch butterfly, but the numbers of monarchs in 2000 showed a 40 per cent increase over the previous year, while the area under GM maize increased by 30 per cent.

GM plants — ancient history?

The testing for foreign genes may reveal some surprising results. Researchers who inserted a gene for resistance to a viral infection into tobacco plants were surprised to discover that similar genes were already present. The plants had been genetically modified by viruses several million years earlier. The virus that infected the ancestor of the tobacco plant left behind a sequence of DNA that may have given the plant resistance to certain viral infections. Since then, the ancestral plant has crossbred with other plants to form the modern tobacco plant.

> ### There should be no release of GM native plants until it can be guaranteed they cannot cross-pollinate with our wild plants.
> Dr Brian Johnson, biotechnology adviser for English Nature

Both organic and conventional farmers would have to buy certified seed each year in order to guarantee uncontaminated seed, rather than save seed. Massive changes in farming practice would be required and there would need to be co-operation between farmers within a region. The changes would push up costs of growing these crops by as much as 40 per cent.

Smart move?

Smart Canola is a very special oil seed rape. It has two genes for weed-killer resistance. It means that farmers can kill off all the weeds using two types of weedkiller, leaving chemically sterilised fields. But Smart Canola is not a GM plant. It has been bred traditionally by selecting characteristics that produced resistance to herbicides. Since it's not GM, it does not need to be put through field trials. Currently its yield is low and this is putting off commercial seed compa-

nies, but this can be easily remedied. All the worries that are being expressed about GM crops apply to Smart Canola. It is likely that this crop could pose just as much threat to wildlife as GM oil seed rape. Yet so far it has failed to attract the public's concern.

The terminator

Scientists are working on a method to make sure that seeds produced by genetically engineered crops are unable to germinate. This has been nicknamed the 'terminator', although a better term is gene protector or GP. This means one seed will produce one plant — any seed saved from the crop will not germinate.

Many people are opposed to these developments. Since the crop plants will not be able to reproduce, farmers will have to buy

Seeds containing a 'terminator' gene would eliminate the risk of modified genes spreading into wild populations of plants, but farmers would have to buy new seed every year.

new seed each year. In many countries, both in Europe and the developing world, farmers traditionally save some of their seed to use the next season. Opponents argue that this technology would put heavy financial pressure on poorer farmers and tie farmers in with the big biotech companies.

The potential producers of GP seed point to farmers who currently use hybrid seed. Hybrid seeds are produced by crossing two parental plants to produce vigorous plants, that produce greater yields. The seeds from hybrid plants do not breed true, so farmers do not save the seed. They have to buy fresh seed each year. They have decided to pay a premium for top quality seed. If GP seed becomes available farmers will decide whether they want to pay more for the new technology. They could still buy non-GP seeds and save seed in the normal way. So far, terminator has only proceeded as far as the patent stage. It will not be ready for commercial use for some years.

The world-wide concern about terminator technology has forced some major biotech companies to withdraw from this area of research. However, there is one major potential benefit for the environment if GP technology is as successful as predicted. If all future GM crops carry GP, there will be virtually no risk of contamination of wild plants with foreign DNA. In the event of a successful cross-pollination between a GM plant with gene protection and a non GM plant, any resulting seeds would be sterile. The environmental impact of such a cross-pollination would therefore be extremely limited and temporary.

Bacteria in a battle against pollution

Much has been made of the risks involved with GM crops, but some genetically engineered bacteria could be extremely useful in our fight to clean up the planet. Over the

The clean-up operation following an oil spill often causes more damage than the oil itself. Oil-digesting bacteria, which break the oil down into harmless sugars would be more environmentally friendly.

years, a great deal of land around the world has been contaminated with toxic and radioactive wastes. Treating this land is not only difficult, but costly. Already, bacteria with natural abilities to digest certain chemicals are being used to clean up industrial sites. More may be done in the future, if we can design bacteria to break down the most poisonous of compounds and render them harmless. Research is already being carried out to improve the naturally occurring bacteria that can 'eat oil', for use following an oil spill. By applying the bacteria to oil-covered beaches, the complex oil molecules would be broken down into harmless sugars.

Mercury pollution is a growing environmental problem. Mercury emissions in Europe alone are expected to increase by thirty per cent within the next ten years. The source of the mercury includes industrial processes, such as the manufacture of chlorine and caustic soda. In developed countries, the amount of mercury released into the environment is strictly controlled. In countries such as Brazil

and Indonesia, migrant workers use mercury to extract gold and there are no controls. Once the mercury enters an aquatic environment, it accumulates through the food chain. People can be poisoned by eating mercury-contaminated fish. New strains of genetically modified bacteria are the latest weapon in the battle to remove mercury from the environment. The bacteria have been altered so that they can take up large amounts of mercury without being poisoned. The mercury-contaminated effluents will pass through treatment tanks where the bacteria will extract the mercury. Water leaving the tanks will be virtually mercury-free. This new method will be much cheaper than using other technologies.

In contrast to the debate on GM crops, the release of genetically engineered bacteria to clean up environmental damage has received little attention. This may be because people cannot see the bacteria. Obviously there is an element of risk when an engineered bacterium is released in the environment, but this risk is probably outweighed by the obvious advantage

Mercury is used to extract gold, but much of it ends up in the water supply where it contaminates fish which may be eaten by humans. GM bacteria have been developed to extract the mercury from the water.

of cleaning up toxic chemicals which would have an even greater effect on the environment.

Saving on resources and energy

Industrial processes are very complex and, when making new chemicals, chemists make use of inorganic catalysts, which speed up chemical reactions. But these catalysts often need high temperatures, and acid or alkaline conditions, in order to work efficiently. In the future, genetically engineered organisms may be able to work effectively at lower temperatures, and require less extreme conditions. This will save money and resources, and will also produce fewer hazardous by-products.

For example, in paper-making, the wood pulp has to be treated with chemicals which break up the fibres and remove the lignin (the substance that makes up wood). The pulp is bleached so that the finished paper is white. This process produces a large volume of chemical waste that has to be treated before it is ready for disposal. Genetic engineering may offer some help. Already, enzymes have been discovered in fungi which may be suitable for use as biological alternatives to some of the chemicals. There are also new strains of trees which contain wood with less lignin, and so require fewer chemicals and less energy to produce the pulp.

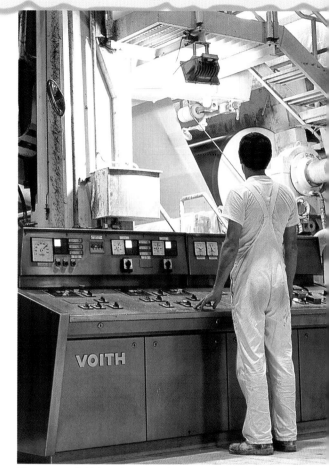

The powerful bleaches used to make paper white may be replaced by enzymes produced by GM fungi.

New sources of oil

Yellow fields of oil seed rape are a common sight, as are blue fields of linseed. Both these crops are grown for their oil, which accumulates in the seeds and fruits of the plants. These oil crops are important sources of renewable oils for pharmaceuticals and cosmetics. While there is still a plentiful supply of cheap fossil-derived oil, the vegetable oil sources are overlooked. But oil will run out within the next fifty to sixty years and then vegetable oils will become increasingly important. Genetic engineering offers scientists the chance to be able to modify oil-producing plants to produce slightly different oils — oils that can be used for specific purposes. These plants will be able to provide a renewable source of oil, one which can be harvested every year. In addition, the crops grow rapidly and use up carbon dioxide,

Oil-producing crops such as oil seed rape and linseed may be modified to produce specific oils for the chemical and the pharmaceutical industries.

which is a greenhouse gas responsible for global warming. Vegetable oils are virtually biodegradable, unlike mineral oils which may contain toxic chemicals such as sulphur and which take many months, often years, to break down when spilt into the environment. Presently as much as thirty per cent of European farmland has been put into 'set-aside' and is out of cultivation due to the overproduction of food in Europe. In future, this land may be used to grow oils.

Plastic is made from oil. Its manufacture uses a lot of energy and produces a variety of polluting by-products. There is now hope that some forms of plastic will be made by living organisms. One biodegradable plastic, called Biopol (trade name), is made by bacteria. One way to make larger quantities of this plastic at lower cost might be to insert the gene into potatoes. This would save on energy, and reduce both cost and pollution. As our supply of fossil fuels (oil, gas and coal) dwindles, we may look to genetically engineered organisms to produce far more materials like plastics.

Face of farming in the future

The way that farmers use herbicide-resistant crops will be crucial to their success. An enlightened farmer could grow GM crops in a way that would benefit wildlife. For example, he might allow weeds to grow a bit longer than normal so that wildlife can take more seeds and insects breed before spraying the crop once with the herbicide. But another farmer might use the herbicide more heavily, destroy all the weeds and create virtual wildlife deserts. No one yet knows how crops with Bt will affect beneficial predators, such as ladybirds. Traditionally, pesticides have been used intermittently, so local populations of insects have a chance to recover. In a GM crop with the Bt gene, the pesticide is there all season long, so it may be necessary to establish Bt-free zones as refuges for insects.

Insects that eat Bt-containing plants do seem to be harmed. We don't really know yet whether the presence of this toxin in our food will have a long-term effect on human health. It may not, but the problem is that we simply do not know, and nothing has yet been done to find out the answer.

The face of farming has changed rapidly in just a few years and the change is still going on. But nobody seems to be asking one fundamental question, 'Why do we need to spray crops with pesticides?' The use of pesticides has only been widespread during the last forty years or so. Before that, farmers managed without, but of course their yields were much smaller. Nowadays farmers can use a variety of approaches to control pests. Instead of using synthetic pesticides, they can use one of the many natural pesticides on the market. Some of these pesticides are selective, for example, natural plant extracts that will damage the external skeletons of insects feed-

The environmental impact has never been an issue here (USA) in the way it has been in Britain. Just as consumer concern has never reached the intensity in evidence in Britain, nobody has taken much notice of what has been happening in relation to the wildlife on farms.
David Green, consultant for the American Soybean Growers' Association, 1999

ing on the crop. Biological pest control has proved to be very successful in Indonesia. Here, farmers were banned from using their favourite pesticide on a major pest of rice, the leaf hopper. This allowed the population of the natural predator to recover. Soon, the farmers discovered that the leaf hopper was on the decline as a result of increased predation. Farmers can also use the technique of inter-cropping, which involves growing several crops in the same field, in alternating rows or blocks. This reduces the ability of pests and diseases to spread through the whole crop.

As the organic movement grows across Europe, there is some evidence that organic farming has the potential to yield just as much as intensive farming. A recent study in the US has shown that the difference in yields between intensively and organically farmed maize over a ten-year period was

Growing rows of different crops makes it difficult for pests and diseases to infect the whole crop.

only one per cent, although some experts say this is an exceptional result. They also argue that organic farming requires more land, which could make large-scale production impractical. (Supporters of organic farming point out that more than thirty per cent of European farmland is now left unused as 'set aside', for which farmers are compensated.)

Nonetheless, modern organic farming could have significant long-term advantages such as increased soil fertility and a positive effect on the surrounding environment. It is possible that the use of GM crops is just one of the options available to a farmer in order to obtain a balance between production and conservation.

5. Pushing back the frontiers of medicine

The news has been full of the new GM foods, but little attention has been paid to the way genetic engineering is helping to overcome disease and is being used to make new medicines which would otherwise be too expensive or difficult to make on a large scale.

Making vaccines

Vaccines have made an important contribution to medical advances, saving the lives of many. Vaccines work by stimulating the immune system. The vaccine does not cause the disease, but it stimulates the body into producing defences so that, when the real virus or bacteria attacks the person, their defences are ready and waiting.

There are various types of vaccine. Some contain micro-organisms that have been killed, but have not lost their ability to trigger an immune response in the body. Others contain micro-organisms that have been weakened so that they do not cause

disease but still induce immunity. These live vaccines tend to produce a better immune response, but very occasionally the micro-organisms change back to a virulent state and cause disease. The latest genetically engineered vaccines do not have this problem.

Genetic engineering enables vaccines to be made quickly, cheaply, in large quantities, and without the need to use animals. DNA is removed from the bacterium which causes the disease, and the gene that codes for a protein is cut out and inserted into the DNA of yeast cells. The yeast cells produce

Flu can be a life-threatening illness in older people. Every winter, people can have a flu vaccination, but its protection only lasts a year.

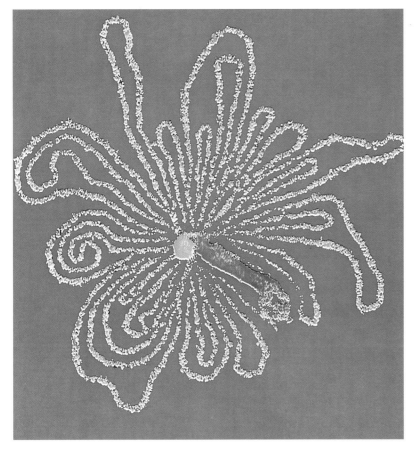

Lengths of DNA extracted from viruses can be used to develop new vaccines.

cells wear away, taking with them all trace of the vaccine and the gold bead carriers. This means that the DNA would only be in the body for a short period of time, so the risk of affecting the body's own DNA is reduced.

Another genetic development could reduce the costs of vaccines and medical teams in developing countries. Various plants have been modified to make the vaccines. One is a genetically modified banana plant. It could be grown in places where the vaccines are needed. People would just need to eat a banana in order to become vaccinated. These developments could save thousands of lives in the poorest parts of the world.

the protein which is used in the vaccine. The presence of bacterial protein is enough to produce an immune response. This method has been used to make vaccines against diseases such as hepatitis B, whooping cough, tetanus and diphtheria.

The way of getting the vaccine into the body may be different in future. One way may be to mix the DNA with a salt solution and then inject it into muscle, where it is absorbed by the cells. Alternatively, doctors may use a 'gene gun'. Microscopic gold beads, covered in the vaccine, are fired at the skin by the gun. The beads lodge just under the surface of the skin, and the vaccine is absorbed into the cells. Eventually, the skin

Fighting rabies

Twenty years ago, rabies in foxes was common across Europe. The foxes spread the disease to both people and dogs. Now, as a result of a vaccination programme, rabies has been virtually eliminated from most of Europe. The rabies vaccine has been genetically engineered using a modified chicken pox virus. Parts of the chicken pox virus were removed and replaced with fragments of genes from the rabies virus. This engineered virus triggered immunity to rabies. Large quantities of the vaccine were produced and mixed with food which was dropped from

Foxes have gained immunity to rabies as a result of eating baited food containing the engineered virus.

the air over a large area in Europe. Foxes ate the baited food and gained immunity — now at least eighty per cent of the fox population is immune to rabies.

Tracy the sheep

Genetic engineering has now made it possible for animals to be modified to make drugs for human use. Some lung and liver diseases can be caused by a lack of the protein alpha-1-antitrypsin, or AAT. Patients can be treated by giving them the AAT that they lack. But AAT is very expensive to make. Large quantities of blood are needed to make just a small amount, and patients need as much as 200g per year. But now there has been a genetic breakthrough. Copies of the human gene which codes for this protein were isolated and transferred to a few sheep embryos. Four female sheep were born, each carrying the gene. These sheep produce the AAT in their milk. One sheep, called Tracy, produces 35g of AAT in every litre of her milk.

So how does the sheep's body know to add

AAT to her milk? A special control gene is inserted at the same time, and it is this second gene that makes sure the AAT gene is only active in the sheep's udders where the milk is made. This way, the AAT is easy to collect, very clean, and easy to purify.

New organ donors

Every year, thousands of people die while they are waiting to receive a new heart or liver. The main problem is a severe shortage of donor organs, and this situation is unlikely to improve. The only way round the problem is either to find a source of artificial organs, or use animal organs.

The main problem with organ transplants is rejection. The patient's body recognises that the new organ is 'foreign', and so the immune system produces antibodies which attack the foreign organ. Unless the patient is given drugs to suppress the immune system, the new organ will be rejected.

Scientists are now trying to genetically engineer pigs so that their organs will not be rejected when placed in a human body. One way is to alter the DNA of the pig so that it grows organs which are covered in human proteins. When these organs are transplanted, the human body is tricked into thinking that the organs are of human origin. The first of this type of genetically engineered pigs have been produced and their organs have been transplanted into monkeys. Unfortunately, the monkeys only survived a short time and so there has been no experimental surgery involving

> In the UK, many people welcome medical applications of gene technology as 'good genetics' but see genetically modified foods as 'bad genetics'.
>
> Bernard Dixon writing in the
> *British Medical Journal* 1999

There will be no shortage of organs for transplants if genetically engineered pigs are used as donors. But will patients accept an organ from a pig?

humans. Another line of research involves the removal of a gene that produces a chemical which causes the human body to reject the organ. The first stage has been achieved with the birth of clone piglets in which the critical gene had been 'knocked out'. However, further genetic manipulation is required to prevent other forms of rejection.

Helping diabetics

When a healthy person eats sugary food, cells in the pancreas secrete insulin. The insulin keeps the blood sugar level steady, regardless of how much food is eaten. Diabetics cannot make enough insulin, so their sugar levels rise and fall steeply, causing many medical problems. They survive by injecting themselves with insulin up to four times a day. Before the development of genetic engineering, insulin was obtained from the bodies of slaughtered cattle and pigs, which caused a number of side-effects. Nowadays, human insulin is made by genetically engineered bacteria.

Genetically inherited childhood diabetes is caused by a defective pancreas. This condition could be overcome by transplanting healthy pancreatic cells into the defective pancreas. However, there is a shortage of suitable human donors and there are many unpleasant side-effects. Animal donors may be the answer. The pig is often used in human genetic engineering, because of its similarities to humans. However, because the number of cells required is so high, it would require 100 pigs to treat just one diabetic. Tilapia fish could be used instead. This tropical fish can be raised in small pools in large numbers. The insulin the fish produces is not the same as human insulin, so some fish have been genetically altered to make human insulin. The human insulin gene is injected into the fish eggs, so that all the young fish carry the human gene. In the future, it is likely that diabetics could receive transplants of pancreatic fish cells.

Tilapia fish grow quickly so could provide a regular supply of pancreatic cells.

Growth hormones

Many other hormones, including human growth hormone, are now made by genetic engineering. Throughout our lives, tiny amounts of human growth hormone are released by the pituitary gland in the brain. It travels in the blood to muscles and bones, where it causes cells to divide and grow. A person who does not produce enough of this hormone is much shorter than normal, often less than 1.2m in height. Unfortunately, growth hormone taken from other animals does not work in humans. So, the only way doctors could get hormone to treat their patients was by extracting it from the pituitary glands of dead people. Since each gland only contains a minute amount, this process was very time consuming and extremely expensive. It took 650 glands to produce just two or three grams of the hormone. At one time, human growth hormone was more expensive than gold of the same weight! Occasionally the hormone was contaminated with a slow-acting virus that killed the recipient. Now, the gene responsible has been inserted into bacteria which produce the human growth hormone. Biotechnology can produce 100 litres of pure growth hormone from bacteria at a fraction of the cost. This is enough to treat the fifty or so children who are born each year with growth hormone deficiency.

Genetic disease

Many millions of people around the world suffer from genetic diseases. Genetic diseases are caused by defective genes, and as many as two out of every three people die from a disorder that is caused, at least in part, by such a defective gene.

There are 4,000 or so genetic disorders that are caused by defects in a single gene, including cystic fibrosis, sickle cell anaemia, muscular dystrophy and phenylketonuria. Most genetic diseases are caused by recessive genes — which means that a person needs to inherit the gene for the disease from both of their parents — so are very rare.

However, many perfectly healthy people are carriers of genetic disorders. They have one normal gene which masks the defective copy of the gene. For example, one person in every 2,000 suffers from cystic fibrosis. But one person in twenty-three actually carries the defective gene.

Fortunately, there are few dominant genetic disorders, such as Huntington's disease. An individual only has to inherit one dominant gene from a parent to suffer from the disease — it is not masked by any other gene. Huntington's disease is characterised by progressive dementia. Unfortunately, this disease only appears in middle age and often the next generation of children carrying the

> **It is the most terrifying disease on the face of the Earth, because its victim is doomed to absolute dementia as terrible as Alzheimer's disease, a loss of physical control akin to muscular dystrophy, and the wasting of the body as bad as the very worst of cancers.**
>
> Milton Wexler, founder of the Hereditary Disease Foundation in Santa Monica, USA, writing about Huntington's disease

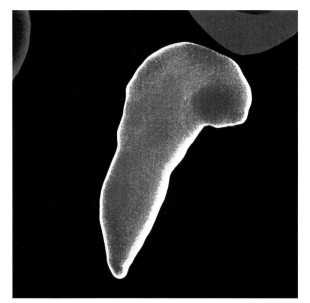

This sickle-shaped red blood cell is caused by a faulty gene, producing the disease sickle cell anaemia. However, these odd-shaped cells give the sufferer resistance to malaria.

> **I don't see that nature has done such a good job that we can't improve on it... it is rather primitive of us to be so fearful of ourselves.**
>
> Fay Weldon, quoted in the *Independent* 1997

dominant gene has already been born.

People suffering from genetic disorders cannot do anything to cure the disease, since every cell of their body carries the disorder. All doctors can do is to treat the symptoms. But genetic engineering — gene therapy — may offer hope to some of these people.

Gene therapy

Gene therapy is a method of treatment which involves taking diseased cells from the patient, altering their DNA, and putting them back into the patient's cells.

Gene therapy has been dramatised in the media, and is often promoted as a miracle cure for all our ailments. But the reality is different. The treatment can only alter faulty genes. If there are no faulty genes, then gene therapy cannot help. It certainly won't change people's personality or IQ, yet it does hold out great promise for people who know they suffer from a genetic disease about which they can currently do nothing.

The first successful gene therapy treatment took place on two girls suffering from the rare genetic disorder called ADA. Because of a faulty gene, their bodies were unable to make a critical enzyme called adenosine deaminase. The disease meant that their white blood cells could not fight disease, leaving their bodies wide open to infection. Until recently, these children would only have survived if they were kept in a germ-free bubble. The new treatment involved taking the human gene for ADA from healthy white blood cells of a donor and inserting the gene into the girls' white blood cells. These changed white blood cells were injected into the bone marrow, where they multiplied to form more white cells, spreading the healthy gene into more and more cells.

The best hope for gene therapy is on diseases which only affect certain parts of the body. ADA treatment was successful because it only involved treating cells in the bone marrow. It will be almost impossible to treat a disease that affects every cell of the body — at least for the foreseeable future.

Treating cystic fibrosis

Cystic fibrosis is a genetic disease that affects the lungs. Sufferers have breathing problems and are prone to lung infections. They have poor digestion and produce abnormally salty sweat. The disease is caused by a defect in a single gene and it affects one in every 2,000 people in the UK. Fifty years ago, eighty per cent of babies with the disease would have died before their first birthday and, even now, few survive beyond their teens.

The faulty gene produces abnormally thick and sticky mucus which clogs up the lungs and blocks ducts into the gut, so enzymes can't reach the food. At the moment, the only form of treatment is to give intense physiotherapy. The sufferer leans over a chair and their back is pummelled to make them cough up the mucus. They also have to take antibiotics, and drugs which relax the muscles in the lungs to make breathing easier.

In 1989, the gene for cystic fibrosis was located. At last, this meant that doctors could start researching a cure. One promising treatment involves the use of an inhaler, similar to those used by asthmatics. When the patient breathes in the spray, it is carried into their lungs where it is absorbed by the lung tissue. The spray contains genetically engineered viruses that invade the lung tissue. These viruses do not cause a disease, but act as a carrier to transfer a new gene into the lung cells. The new gene allows the cell to make normal mucus. Unfortunately, the cells have a limited life, so the treatment would have to be repeated throughout the patient's life.

A similar treatment involving the use of viruses received a major setback when one patient in a group of eighteen taking part in a trial died. The treatment used a virus to switch on the production of an essential enzyme in

A doctor measures the lung capacity of a cystic fibrosis sufferer.

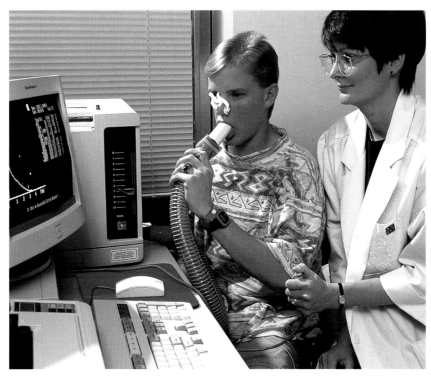

the liver. The patient receiving the highest dose of viruses died and the trial has been stopped.

Fixing the genes

The rare genetic disease, Crigler-Najjar, is common amongst the Amish people of Lancaster County, Pennsylvania. The disease is caused by a single faulty code in the gene for a critical liver enzyme. The enzyme breaks down bilirubin, a toxic waste product from the destruction of old red blood cells. Without the enzyme, the bilirubin builds up to toxic levels, causing liver disease and finally death. The Amish people normally shun technology, but children who have the condition are allowed to sleep under a special blue light that destroys the bilirubin. If this doesn't work, the child has to have a liver transplant.

A new technique has been developed to repair the faulty gene. Patients will be injected with microscopic fat globules containing molecules of DNA. This DNA will bind to the defective length of DNA in such a way that repair enzymes in the cell repair the fault.

In tests on rats, up to twenty per cent of the liver cells were repaired using this method.

Detecting DNA diseases

As our knowledge of human DNA improves, it will become possible to check a person's DNA during a routine medical check-up. The genes for many diseases have already been identified, and their DNA sequences worked out. It is now quite routine in the genetics laboratory to check somebody's DNA to see if just one base in 6,000,000,000 is abnormal, indicating whether or not a person carries a specific genetic disease. Doctors can even test cells taken from an embryo just a few hours old. This test is called genetic screening. People can be screened for genetic diseases such as muscular dystrophy, cystic fibrosis, Huntingdon's disease, some breast cancers, Tay-Sachs disease and sickle cell anaemia. However, all this means at the moment is that we know if somebody has the disease.

One reason that cystic fibrosis is so common is that parents do not know that they are carrying a gene for the disease. If only one parent has the gene, the children will be

Cell-specific

Most human cells contain twenty-three identical pairs of chromosomes. The chromosomes carry the genes. A defective gene will be found in all the cells of the body, but it will only cause a problem in those cells that use the gene. For example, the gene for cystic fibrosis causes faulty mucus secretion. It causes a problem in cells in the liver, pancreas and lungs — the organs which produce mucus. Gene therapy to treat this disease has to be directed at these affected areas.

unaffected. But if both parents carry the gene, there is a one in four chance that their child will have cystic fibrosis. Because the gene has now been identified, genetic screening for cystic fibrosis is already possible. The parents give a blood sample and the DNA is extracted and examined. Doctors can then advise the parents of the risks to any child.

Dyslexia, too may have a genetic origin. Researchers working on this reading disorder have homed in on two chromosomes which may carry the defective gene. They are studying the DNA of families in which there is a high incidence of dyslexia. It is likely that more than one gene is involved. Once the research is complete, it is likely that there will be a genetic test for the condition.

The ageing effects of eating

Research into the genome of the mouse has made some exciting discoveries about ageing. As the body ages, chromosomes become damaged and this affects the genes. If chromosome damage could be limited, the ageing processes could be slowed down and even halted.

Working with mice, the scientists have compiled a genetic map of ageing. This is based on the genes that change with age, especially those involved in stress responses, protein repair and energy production. They have discovered that a low-calorie diet can extend life and preserve health. A low calorie diet slows the body's metabolism — the rate at which it ticks over — and reduces stress responses.

> **The available evidence suggests that at present there is no demand for the genetic testing of employees, though the possibility of more widespread use in the future should not be ruled out.**
> The Nuffield Council on Bioethics

Some breast cancers are caused by a faulty gene. This gene can be passed down the generations, from mother to daughter.

These young Chinese school children will have to undergo genetic screening before they can marry or have children.

Gene technology was at the centre of this research. About ten per cent of the genetic code of the mouse was examined, using a revolutionary 'gene chip'. This is a small glass plate containing DNA that, when read with a laser, reveals the activity of thousands of genes. The activity of genes in mice fed on a normal diet was compared with that of mice fed on a low-calorie diet. They discovered that a small number of genes had changed in the mice eating the normal diet, but the same genes were intact in mice on the calorie-reduced diet. Armed with this knowledge, researchers can develop drugs which mimic the age-retarding effects of a low calorie diet.

Passport to health?

There are both advantages and disadvantages in genetic screening. It will allow us to know whether we are likely in the future to develop certain genetic diseases. In years to come, we may even carry a genetic passport which identifies all the diseases to which we may be susceptible. As this becomes more widespread, companies may ask people to undergo genetic screening in the same way they currently have routine physical health checks. One danger is that people with faulty genes may be unable to get health insurance or jobs.

Some fear that people wishing to have a child or get married may be required to be tested to see if they have a clean bill of health. This is already happening in China, where the law requires that couples who wish to get married undergo screening for some genetic diseases, infectious diseases, and mental disorders. If one of the couple is found to have the wrong genes, they can only marry if they agree to sterilisation or long-term contraception.

Designer babies?

Among the most contentious issues facing society today are human cloning and altering human DNA. The Human Genome Project has provided scientists with knowledge of the genetic code. Scientists can alter DNA in order to cure genetic diseases, but they could alter DNA in order to selectively change a person's characteristics. Already gene technology companies have developed techniques to genetically alter sperm cells in animals so that certain traits are inherited in the offspring. Soon it could be possible to do this with human sperm cells. This technique may be used to remove defective genes and so prevent a child inheriting a genetic disease. But if the technology existed it would be difficult to stop sperm being altered to eliminate unwanted genes, or indeed to replace genes. Similar techniques could be developed to alter genes in embryos. Currently, human reproductive cloning (the creation of a genetically identical copy of a living person) is not allowed in any country. In the UK, human embryos may be used in medical research and allowed to develop until they are 14 days old, then they must be destroyed.

One of the key techniques in human cloning is *in vitro* fertilisation (IVF). IVF involves removing eggs from a woman and fertilising them externally. This produces a number of embryos. One or two of these embryos are replaced in the woman's uterus and the pregnancy continues as normal. Any unused embryos are normally stored at -173°C in case the first attempt does not succeed. IVF is usually used to help couple who for various reasons are infertile, but it is also used to produce embryos for research and in the future could be used for cloning.

Since human reproductive cloning is banned, the information that follows is based

> **The idea that most of us are perfect is simply wrong... On average everybody in Britain carries one or perhaps even two defective genes.**
> Steve Jones, Professor of Genetics at University College London

on theory. The process of producing a human clone would take place in the following way. An egg cell would be stripped of its nucleus. A nucleus would be taken from the donor cell and inserted into the empty egg cell. A small electric current would be passed through the cell in order to get it to start dividing and form an embryo. The embryo would be allowed to grow for a few days and then placed in the uterus of a surrogate mother. The resulting child would be a genetic copy of the donor. Although this process sounds relatively straightforward, in reality, it is incredibly complex and there is a high failure rate. The researchers that produced Dolly the Sheep tried fusing the egg cell with the donor nucleus hundreds of times before they managed to get a few embryos. Only one of the embryos grew into a sheep and was born. In the case of human clones, researchers would need access to hundreds of human eggs. And even if researchers overcame the problems of producing embryos, there is no guarantee that the clone would be healthy. It could be born with defects or have some form of disability as a result of the cloning process.

Human cloning raises issues concerned with the welfare and identity of the clone. A child that is identical to another person may not be treated as a unique individual. They may be expected to have the same character, abilities and interests as the older clone, just because they look the same. However, characteristics such as personality and intelligence are affected by the way a person grows up, their family and their surroundings. Human cloning could offer some hope to infertile couples who cannot be helped by conven-

Laboratory mice are the most commonly used animals for genetic experiments.

tional IVF treatment. For example, a woman who could not produce healthy eggs could use eggs from a donor. A nucleus from one of her cells would replace the nucleus in the donor egg. Many people may think that this would be acceptable. But there is also the possibility that a person could produce a clone of themselves, or a sick child, purely for the purpose of supplying organs for an essential transplant operation.

The only way to stop the possibility of human cloning is to stop all research into human embryos. But this would mean that many promising medical developments would be halted too. Governments in many countries are debating this issue. In the UK, the government decided that research into human embryos would be allowed to continue up to

14 days, as the benefits from the research outweighed the risks. Today there are strict rules controlling research. In contrast, the House of Representatives in the US has voted to ban all human cloning so medical research using human embryos may not take place.

Life without end?

It is possible that the human genome project will reveal facts about certain genes that some would consider better left undiscovered. What if scientists found that certain genes determined how long we lived? Perhaps there would be 'designer oldies' — older people who undergo regular genetic clean-ups to remove ageing genes. Although this seems unthinkable now, one thing seems certain: if scientists do discover this, or similar, information, it will be difficult to stop some people from using (or abusing) it.

It is interesting to note that there has been very little in the press about the use of GM technology in medicine. It is already clear that many people do not want to eat GM foods, but how many realise that life-saving vaccines and other drugs are produced by GM organisms? Cheap vaccines will soon be available to people living in the developing world, where they will have the potential to save millions of lives. There is some debate about the ethics of using pigs as organ donors, but do the desire for and benefits of using GM donor organs to cure, say, heart disease outweigh the ethical considerations?

The medical advances in the field of gene therapy raise just as many moral and ethical questions. No individual is perfect and many of us would no doubt prefer certain features to be different. But given the chance to make change, would we take that chance? If we did, would we make changes to conform to the current ideal model? In the 1600s, women with a generously curved body were thought to be more desirable that thin women. How would we change our bodies today? Do we want to live in a 'designer world'?

There is, of course, a significant risk of abuse in this area. In a world where money speaks, it is highly likely that some rich parents would demand that genetic modifications were carried out on their unborn child to make them perfect, at least in their eyes. But who is to be the arbiter of their judgement, and what happens if it goes wrong? What happens to the child, and who would be to blame? What would we do if a research institute produced

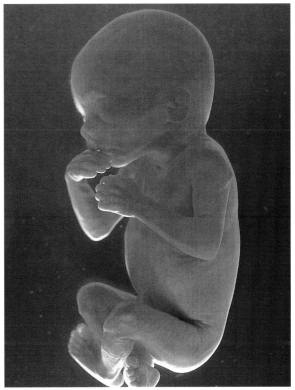

Do we want to be able to alter the genes of an unborn child?

a cloned baby? Would the baby have any rights? Would it be owned by the institute? This may all seem far-fetched, belonging more to science fiction than our world, but the future may be with us sooner than we think, for the technology to do this is not very far away.

In the future, there is a real prospect of GM technology allowing us to continually repair damaged cells, allowing people to live forever. This raises yet another question. Would we really want to be immortal?

6. The genetic battlefield

During the 1970s and 1980s, one of the public's biggest concerns was nuclear energy and weapons. Today, it is genetic engineering that's hitting the headlines. Genetic engineering affects our daily lives — our food, our environment and our health. These issues do not just affect Europe and North America — they are global issues.

In many cases it's not the science that worries people, but the way that it is applied. There are concerns that the new technology is in the hands of a few giant multi-national companies that are seen as more interested in making money and controlling their markets than protecting the rights of farmers and consumers. The major agrochemical companies operate in every country and their marketing decisions affect every farmer, from peasant farmers working a few hectares to the rich grain barons of Europe and North America. In court rooms across the world, the biotech companies are claiming ownership of DNA and gene sequences.

> **People are in this game to make money, and if they can't protect their discovery they won't bother to make discoveries at all.**
> Steve Jones, Professor of Genetics at University College, London

Staking a claim

The issue of ownership of genes is critical. The companies staking their claims say that the finding, removal, and alteration of a gene is a scientific invention. Opponents believe that it is immoral to claim ownership over an organism's DNA.

If it is a true scientific invention, then companies or individuals have the right to protect that invention through the international patent system. This system dates back hundreds of years. If you are an inventor and you produce something new and commercially valuable, you can protect your idea by getting a patent. This gives you exclusive rights to your invention for twenty years. A competitor cannot steal your idea and make money from it. In return, you must publish details of your idea. Everybody can read about your invention and see how it works, but they may not use it without your permission.

The only other way of protecting your invention is to keep it a secret. If your idea was stolen, and another company started using it, you would not be able to stop them. In fact, they might even patent your idea themselves, and then prevent you from using it.

Companies developing genetically engineered organisms want protection for their work, which is incredibly expensive. They contend that the only way to get protection is to own a patent on the organism. As a result, they are busy trying to convince the courts that they are producing true scientific inventions, and not simply a discovery of something that was already there.

Already, one patent office has made an interesting ruling. A DNA sequence was discovered (a fact that would not itself have been patentable), but the company went on to invent a method of extracting and replicating the DNA, and the patent office ruled that a patent could be granted for the invention of the process. In August 1999, Advanced Cell Technology (ACT) in the USA was granted the first major patent on cloning mammals from specialised fetal or adult cells. The Roslin Institute in Scotland, which created Dolly the sheep, has several patents pending for cloning techniques.

Many groups of people disagree with this whole principle, and are particularly concerned about the patenting of human DNA. They argue that, since DNA is found in every one of us, the best way forward would be to make sure that all the information, including that discovered by the Human Genome Project, is owned collectively by the people and not by individuals. Members of the European Parliament claim that human genes are the same as human life, and that patenting a gene is therefore immoral. However, the European Patent Office has disagreed and has decided that it is possible to patent human genes.

One controversial case involves two genes linked to breast cancer. A medical research company has filed for patents which would prevent other medical researchers working on these genes for commercial gain. Much of the basic research into these genes was carried out by several medical research institutes. Opponents to these patents claim that the company did not use a novel process and therefore a patent should not be issued.

There are currently hundreds of patents approved or pending for genetically engineered animals, including fish, cows, mice and pigs. Many more patents, concerned with plants and bacteria, are also in the pipeline.

Biopiracy

Most of the new genetically engineered crops and drugs contain genes taken from wild species of bacteria, fungi, plants and animals. All the major biotech companies are spending billions of pounds in their search for new sources of genes. They have set up research centres in many countries to analyse native plant species for useful characteristics. Once discovered, the genes are inserted into crops which are marketed by the biotech companies. Unfortunately, very little of the profit returns to the country of origin.

Under the Convention on Biodiversity, signed by many nations at the Earth Summit in 1992 (though not by the USA), royalty payments should be made on products derived from indigenous species. The agreement thought of 'species rights' similarly to intellectual property rights. Unfortunately, these royalty payments are not being made. In 1994, a report for the United Nations Development Programme estimated that developing countries lost up to

> **Monsanto first described the terminator as a patent, then a conceptual patent, then a prophetic patent. If so, it's a nightmare prophesy.**
> Dr Vandana Shiva, scientist and farmers' advocate in India

$5.4 billion each year from royalty payments on new drugs and agricultural products derived from indigenous plants.

While the biotech companies are very protective of their intellectual property rights, they have yet, it seems, to take the same care over ensuring that developing world nations receive their just dues from their 'species rights'.

The case of Basmati rice

Many countries are now looking for legal ways of protecting their own indigenous plants and varieties of crops. Currently, Indian farmers are facing a threat to their best known variety of rice — the Basmati rice. Basmati rice is the champagne of rice varieties. It has been grown by Indian farmers for hundreds of years and during that time they have improved the rice.

> **The new life [science] industry has become commercially transgenic, allowing one company to span pharmaceuticals, crop chemicals, plants and animal breeding, veterinary medicines and even food processing.**
> Rural Advancement Foundation International 1999, a non-governmental organisation based in Canada dedicated to conservation and sustainable improvement of agricultural biodiversity

There are almost thirty different varieties of Basmati and it makes up fifteen per cent of the total Indian rice crop. In 1997, a US-based company was granted a patent on certain Basmati varieties, to include the plants and seeds. Although the patent is on a newly developed variety, the essential Basmati genes are derived from seeds produced by Indian farmers. This patent also seeks to protect varieties which are functionally equivalent. This means that Indian farmers developing new varieties of their own could be infringing the patent. India does not allow patents on life forms and the government is opposing the patent on legal grounds and on the grounds that it threatens India's culture, science, heritage and economy. India has now set up a programme to develop a database of everything that is known about traditional medicines, which will be available to everybody. By making sure that all the information is in the public domain and classified as 'prior knowledge', India is ensuring that companies will be unable to patent traditional medicines.

Saving seed — illegal

If you buy a packet of seeds from a shop and grow them you can, if you wish, take cuttings or save the new seeds to make more plants for next year. But this is not legal if you have bought a packet of genetically engineered seeds because it is sold to you under a special licence that protects the seed producer's rights. The only way you are allowed to obtain new plants is to buy more seed.

Traditionally, farmers around the world save some of their harvest to use as next year's seed, unless they are using certain types of conventionally bred crops which give better yields but which do not produce fertils seeds. At the moment, eighty per cent of crops planted in the developing world are

Of trees and turmeric

The Indian neem tree grows throughout the sub-continent and has extraordinary medicinal properties. For hundreds of years, people have made use of almost every part of the tree. Leaves of the neem are stored with grain to keep insects away, while leaf extracts are used to stop infections, keep mosquitoes away, and even act as a contraceptive. Its twigs can be used as a toothbrush, because it stops tooth decay.

Companies in the developed world have discovered many of its active ingredients, and are using neem extracts in dental and skin care products and insecticides. They are applying for patents to protect those products and make money. However, the people of India, who have known about the neem for many years, seem to be in danger of losing out to commercial interests, and may well receive little real benefit from this remarkable tree.

Turmeric has been used for generations in India to treat cuts and wounds, but a US university has recently been granted a patent on the wound-healing abilities of turmeric. That patent gives the university a monopoly over such uses.

from saved seed. Even in the UK, farmers often save as much as thirty per cent of their crop for use the following season. With genetically engineered seed, this is prevented under the terms of the licence.

The reason for this is, quite simply, economics. The companies developing the genetically engineered plants spend many millions of pounds in development, and they certainly don't want other people selling or propagating their plants or it wouldn't be worth them investing in the research in the first place. They need to be able to control the use of these new plants, in order to protect their investments. If the GM seeds are used, they will lock all farmers, poor and better-off alike, into tightly controlled marketing and licence arrangements. The farmers will become totally dependent on the seed and chemical manufacturer.

Supporters of GM crops say that many farmers choose to buy fresh seed each year — and this is true. Farmers growing high-yielding hybrid crops do not save seed. The quality of saved seed from hybrid plants cannot be guaranteed, so the farmers buy fresh seed. However, this is generally more commonplace in North America and Europe than in the developing world. The long-term problem is one of choice. As more GM varieties come to the marketplace, the non-GM seeds may be squeezed out. This will leave the farmers with little choice.

Feeding the world

The world's population is growing. There are six billion people living on the planet

> In order to find lasting solutions to world food problems, we need to work with sustainable agricultural processes which do not pose threats to the environment and human and animal health. Genetic engineering, like the so-called 'green revolution', is just another short-term dangerous attempt to provide a quick fix. It does not address the real problems of world famine.
>
> Greenpeace statement

and within the next twenty or thirty years the population may rise to eight billion. The GM companies claim that their new crops will help to feed the world. But is this true? What is undeniable is that 800 million people are malnourished. But this is not always through a lack of food. In fact, 8 out of 10 malnourished children live surrounded by food surpluses. In most cases, the cause is poverty - people are too poor to afford food. This huge problem could be solved by a massive redistribution of food, but realistically, this is unlikely to happen. So other measures are needed. In many countries, the yields from many staple crops are poor, so the farmer receives a low income which results in poverty. Poor farmers cannot afford to employ anybody on their land and this leads to higher levels of unemployment and more poverty. Arguably, GM crops could help these farmers raise their income, without the need to buy expensive pesticides. As farming income increases, the level of unemployment falls and the whole community benefits.

The majority of the existing GM crops have been modified not to increase yield but to provide protection against pests and weed-killers. This means that a farmer growing these crops benefits from the reduced costs of fertilisers and pesticides. The biotech companies have focussed on mainstream economic crops such as maize, soybean, cotton, rubber and papaya. GM seed is relatively expensive to buy so GM crops are grown mostly in developed countries. However, most of the developing world rely on staple crops such as plantain, cassava, sorghum and millet. These crops are grown on small farms by farmers who cannot afford to buy fertilisers and pesticides. Unfortunately these crops suffer badly from disease and pests and as a result their yield is quite low. But they have the potential to yield much more. For example, cassava yields less than 8 tonnes per acre, but the potential yield could be as much as 80 tonnes. Over the last

A farm in southern Bangladesh is totally surrounded by flood waters after being hit by a cyclone. Can GM crops help farmers in the developing world?

30 years, as a result of conventional breeding programmes wheat has shown a 130 per cent increase in average yields. In this time the yield of cassava has improved by barely 3 per cent. More than 600 million people rely on cassava as their staple food. Imagine the benefits if the yield of this crop was improved. Now that really would help to feed more people! But it needs a change in policy for the biotech companies to work on the less profitable crops of the developing world.

The new GM crops may also threaten the traditional markets of the developing

> We object strongly that the image of the poor and hungry from our countries is being used by giant multinational corporations to push a technology that is neither safe, environmentally friendly, nor economically beneficial to us.
>
> Statement by delegates to the UN FAO from 24 African states

> **Much of the research on genetically modified organisms is not dealing with the right crops or the right problems within these crops to benefit developing countries.**
>
> Lynn Mytelka, Director of United Nations University Institute for New Technologies, 2002.

world. By altering tropical crops so that they can be grown in temperate areas such as Europe and the US, tropical countries will lose exports, and hence both income for farmers and foreign currency with which to pay off overseas debt. However, if traditional farmers were to switch to organic methods, they might well see an increase in income, for there is a burgeoning organic market now developing in many developed countries.

Farmers in the developing world have already begun to realise this. In Chile, organic fruit exports have grown by 400 per cent, while Ugandan organic cotton is now twenty per cent more profitable than that which is grown using pesticides. Ironically, while it is in the developing countries that pesticides have been most mis-used, a switch to organic farming in these places may be the saving of the farmers' livelihoods, as well as helping the environment.

Biodiversity

Over the last fifty years, at least three quarters of the world's food plant varieties have vanished as farmers have concentrated on

▶ A wide range of rice varieties are undergoing trials at Indian crop research institutes. It is important that as many varieties of rice as possible are maintained for future use.

> **The five major agrochemical companies envisage a future where only a handful of varieties of wheat, maize, rice and other food crops are grown commercially. They are working flat out to ensure that within a decade most of the world's staple crops will be from genetically modified seed which they have engineered. As a result, few traditional varieties will be available to farmers. These new strains will only be available from them, at their price. They will be resistant to the most powerful herbicide which farmers will use to kill every other plant in the field, producing a chemical desert devoid of wildlife.**
>
> Patrick Holden, Director of the Soil Association, 1999

a few commercial strains. Even in the UK, traditional varieties of seeds have been lost, because seed producers have to pay to licence the varieties they wish to sell. If the varieties

> **The application of genetic modification to crops has the potential to bring about significant benefits, such as improved nutrition, enhanced pest resistance, increased yields and new products such as vaccines. The moral imperative for making GM crops readily and economically available to developing countries who want them is compelling. The Working Party recommends a major increase in financial support for GM crop research directed at the employment-intensive production of food staples together with the implementation of international safeguards.**
>
> Working Party report on genetically modified crops — the ethical and social issues, Nuffield Council on Bioethics 1999

are not commercially viable, they drop the seed. The end result is fewer seed types and a resultant reduction in genetic diversity.

Across the world as a whole, we are moving inexorably towards a global dependence on a very small range of crops. In 1900, for example, there were 30,000 varieties of rice in India, but this number has declined rapidly. In 1970, the few modern variants in use were all attacked by disease. While there was a group of traditional rice varieties that showed resistance to this disease, nothing was done to conserve them and these traditional varieties have now become extinct.

Genetic uniformity carries huge risks and makes our dependence on agrochemicals exceedingly worrying. Intensive, large-scale farming increases vulnerability by allowing disease to spread easily and it reduces the range of plants that might evolve to suit new conditions in the future.

A changing market place

The agrochemical market is changing. Today, eighty-five per cent of the global agrochemical market is controlled by ten companies and the top five alone control almost the entire global GM seed market. These multinational enterprises are steadily getting bigger and more powerful, as they take over smaller companies and buy land. Already, they own more land in Brazil than the peasant farmers. These companies have invested billions of pounds in their technology and, not unreasonably, they want a return on their investment. Their marketing strategy is affecting farming and food around the world.

GM crop trials are often carried out in developing countries. This is because crops need field trials where they are to be farmed, although some people argue it is because of the very stringent controls and regulatory approvals required in Europe. However, once the test and development process is completed, global trade agreements such as GATT (the General Agreement on Tariffs and Trades) mean that trade in new GM crops cannot be prevented. It often seems that governments no longer have the right to choose what is imported into their own country — banning GM crops because they 'might damage health' is not terribly convincing to international courts. Another area for concern is the global nature of the problem. The world-wide planting of GM soya, for example, may mean that UK consumers would have no choice but to accept GM soya; there would be no GM-free source.

The world over, an increasing number of disputes are breaking out over the regulation and sale of GMOs and the rights to genes. Trade wars have become a real possibility as the EU and Japan attempt to ban certain GM crop imports. Trade and biodiversity agreements, such as that signed at the Earth Summit, and world trade agreements, such as GATT, create natural tensions. The Convention on Biodiversity was designed to stop people exploiting the genetic resources of other countries, while trade agreements act to ensure that cross-border trade is unrestricted.

The big decision

One big issue can be summed up by a simple question: Should any organisation have the right to 'own' a natural resource? The battle lines have already been drawn. Multinational companies, backed by the USA, want to allow the patenting of organisms in order that commercial development can continue, while many nations, backed by concerned environmentalists, want to protect their natural resources through the introduction of rights over their indigenous species, and outlaw patenting of gene sequences.

'Agricultural biotechnology... holds great promise for Africa and other areas of the world where circumstances such as poverty and poor growing conditions make farming difficult ... starving people ... want food and nourishment, not lectures, and we certainly won't allow ourselves to be intimidated by eco-terrorists who destroy crops and disrupt scientific meetings ... We will proceed carefully and thoughtfully, but we want to have the opportunity to save the lives of millions of people and change the course of history in many nations.

from a statement by Hassan Adamu, Nigerian Minister of Agriculture and Rural Development'

HRH the Prince of Wales versus Professor Derek Burke: 10 Questions

HRH the Prince of Wales has made no secret of his concerns about genetic engineering. On 1 June 1999, the Daily Mail published the following ten questions posed by the Prince.

Professor Derek Burke, a former chairman of the Government's Advisory Committee on Novel Foods and Processes, has produced a response to the 10 questions which were posed by the Prince of Wales.

1. Do we need GM food in this country?

On the basis of what we have seen so far, we don't appear to need it at all. The benefits, such as there are, seem to be limited to the people who own the technology and the people who farm on an industrialised scale. We are constantly told that this technology may have huge benefits for the future. Well, perhaps. But we have all heard claims like that before and they don't always come true in the long run — look at the case of antibiotic growth promoters in animal feedstuff.

Not now, you may say; we have enough. But food has become cheaper, and better throughout my life — I grew up in a family where chicken was an annual treat — because farmers have used every new technology to our benefit. We can do the same with GM and use the higher yields to stop using marginal land and to restore the hills and coastal strips to their natural state. And when have we British turned our backs on a new technology? New technologies are not all good or all bad: they change things and they pose new questions. So why should we run away from GM?

2. Is GM food safe for us to eat?

There is certainly no evidence to the contrary. But how much evidence do we have? And are we looking at the right things? The major decisions about what can be grown and what can be sold are taken

Just what is the basis for treating GM foods as so intrinsically dangerous that they should be regarded as the Devil's concoction? Why so black and white? Of course it would

on the basis of studying what is known about the original plant, comparing it to the genetically modified variety, and then deciding whether the two are 'substantially equivalent'. But is it enough to look only at what is already known? Isn't there at least a possibility that the new crops (particularly those that have been made resistant to antibiotics) will behave in unexpected ways, producing toxic or allergic reactions? Only independent scientific research, over a long period, can provide the final answer.

be possible to make GM 'food' that was dangerous, but I contend that the three GM foods approved for sale in the UK — cheese, tomato paste and soya — are as safe to eat as any other, and I have no hesitation in doing so. Why not treat food on its merits?

3. Why are the rules for approving GM foods so much less stringent than those for new medicines produced using the same technology?

Before drugs are released into the marketplace they have to undergo the most rigorous testing — and quite right too. But GM food is also designed in a laboratory for human consumption, albeit in different circumstances. Surely it is equally important that we are confident that they will do us no harm?

This is a 'when did you stop beating your wife' question. The answer has already been given in the question. The answer is clear: the rules are not less stringent, they are different and the same as used elsewhere in the world. Drugs are tested on animals at hundreds of times their clinical doses; that is not possible with food, so different ways have been devised. But if you really want to start trials in humans, 300 million Americans have been eating GM soya for several years now without any ill effects.

4. How much do we really know about the environmental consequences of GM crops?

Laboratory tests showing that pollen from GM maize in the United States caused damage to the caterpillars of Monarch butterflies provide the latest cause for concern. If GM plants can do this to butterflies, what damage might they cause to other species? But more alarmingly perhaps, this GM maize is not under test. It is already being grown commercially throughout large areas of the United States of America. Surely this effect should have been discovered by the company producing the seeds, or the regulatory authorities who approved them for sale, at a much earlier stage? Indeed, how much more are we going to learn the hard way about the impact of GM crops on the environment?

A huge area — one and a half times the size of Britain — is now sown with GM in North America and, although the environment is not the same, there have been no big problems. The well publicised experiments with the Monarch butterfly show that under laboratory conditions caterpillars force-fed corn pollen are damaged, but it is unlikely that in the wild the caterpillars would eat corn pollen at all. The effect is real and needs to be guarded against but it is not the catastrophe that some claim.

5. Is it sensible to plant test crops without strict regulations in place?

Such crops are being planted in this country now — under a voluntary code of practice. But English Nature, the Government's official adviser on nature conservation, has argued that we ought to put strict, enforceable regulations in place first. Even then, will it really be possible to prevent contamination of nearby wildlife or crops, whether organic or not? Since bees and the wind don't obey any sort of rules — voluntary or statutory — we shall soon have an unprecedented and unethical situation in which one farmer's crops will contaminate another's against his will.

We already have EU regulations which have the force of law. Now we are using a voluntary code of practice that goes beyond EU rules, is voluntary because we don't want to wait for the EU, and which is overseen by an independent body recently appointed by the minister. We need these trials so that real choices can be made about appropriate regulation, and so it is important that vandals do not destroy them and that farmers are not put under pressure by green groups to abandon them.

6. How will consumers be able to exercise genuine choice?

Labelling schemes clearly have a role to play. But if conventional and organic crops can become contaminated by GM crops grown nearby, those people who wish to be sure they are eating or growing absolutely natural, non-industrialised, real food, will be denied that choice. This seems to me to be wrong.

Consumers had choice over the first two products, and only when GM soya was introduced was choice lost. Now the emotional campaign against GM foods has removed choice for those of us who want to eat GM soya. So who is being autocratic now? I noticed too that the Prince has removed choice from those farmers who farm on his land. Why don't the farmers have choice like US farmers do? There is absolutely no evidence of risk.

7. If something goes wrong with a GM crop, who would be held responsible?

It is important that we know precisely who is going to be legally liable to pay for any damage — whether it be to human health, the environment, or both. Will it be the company who sells the seed or the farmer who grows it? Or will it, as was the case with BSE, be all of us?

Exactly the same bodies as before; for we have been introducing new crops for years —[oilseed] rape and short-stalked wheat, for example — and there have always been mechanisms for dealing with any damage. To pretend otherwise is misleading.

8. Are GM crops really the only way to feed the world's growing population?

This argument sounds suspiciously like emotional blackmail to me. Is there any serious academic research to substantiate such a sweeping statement? The countries which might be expected to benefit certainly take a different view. Representatives of 20 African states, including Ethiopia, have published a statement denying that gene technologies will 'help farmers to produce

No one has ever said it was, but it seems perverse, even criminal, to walk away from an increased source of food when we need it desperately. And it can help; a new rice with increased vitamin A and iron content is almost ready to meet a huge need in South-East Asia.

the food that is needed in the 21st Century'. On the contrary, they 'think it will destroy the diversity, the local knowledge and the sustainable agricultural systems… and undermine our capacity to feed ourselves'. How much more could we achieve if all the research funds currently devoted to fashionable GM techniques — which run into billions of dollars a year — were applied to improving methods of agriculture which have stood the test of time? We already know that yields from many traditional farming systems can be doubled, at least, by making better use of existing natural resources.

9. What effect will GM crops have on people of the world's poorest countries?

Christian Aid has just published a devastating report, entitled *Selling Suicide*, explaining why GM crops are unlikely to provide solutions to the problems of famine and poverty. Where people are starving, lack of food is rarely the underlying cause. It is more likely to be lack of money to buy food, distribution problems or political difficulties. The need is to create sustainable livelihoods for everyone. Will GM crops really do anything to help? Or will they make the problems worse, leading to increasingly industrialised forms of agriculture, with larger farms, crops grown for export while indigenous populations starve, and more displaced farm workers heading for a miserable, degraded existence in yet more shanty towns?

The Nuffield Council on Bioethics in its recent report points out that, with care, this new technology can help the poorest; a challenge that it is unwise, I suggest even immoral, to walk away from.

10. What sort of world do we want to live in?

This is the biggest question of all. I raise it because the capacity of GM technology to change our world has brought us to a crossroads of fundamental importance. Are we going to allow the industrialisation of Life itself, redesigning the natural world for the sake of convenience and embarking on an Orwellian future? And, if we do, will there eventually be a price to pay? Or should we be adopting a gentler, more considered approach, seeking always to work with the grain of Nature in making better, more sustainable use of what we have, for the long-term benefit of mankind as a whole? The answer is important. It will affect far more than the food we eat; it will determine the sort of world we, and our children, inhabit.

I do not want either of the Prince's worlds; neither the Orwellian future nor his organic world, and fortunately for nearly everyone there are many other choices. I want a world where we use technology safely and constructively and we can do that if we keep our heads, which at the moment we are signally failing to do.

Conclusion: The genetic revolution — good or bad?

The genetic revolution started in 1953 when Francis Crick and James Watson worked out the molecular structure of DNA. Today, scientists are on the verge of unravelling the structure of every gene in the human body.

The recent developments in gene technology represent a giant step forward. Now we have the ability to change the blueprint of life itself. However, the techniques of genetic engineering are relatively crude and haphazard. Dolly was proclaimed a great step forward. The fact that hundreds of previous attempts had failed was not reported by the media. Scientists can take a gene from a fish and put it into a strawberry plant to create a frost-resistant fruit. But they really do not know what effect this change in genetic make-up will have on the other genes and the organism's life span. We must never lose sight of the fact that life is complex and has the unfailing capacity to surprise.

What's the hurry?

Some people are calling for a five-year moratorium on GM development and patenting, to allow further research into the potential benefits and threats of GM to people in both the developed and developing world, while others want to push ahead with the new developments.

One of the key factors in this debate has been the lack of information and research results. Millions of people are eating GM foods without any apparent adverse effect on their health. However, others would argue that it is too early to assess any long-term effects on health and biodiversity. Members of the public need to be able to trust their governments and scientists. This can be achieved by making sure that there is access to information on monitoring, research results and safety assessments. Then everybody can make their own choice.

GM is a global issue. Hence there has to be international debate. Another global issue, climate change, has been tackled by governments setting up the International Panel on Climate Change, where governments and non-governmental organisations have grouped together to face the problem. A similar panel could be set up to oversee the developments in the field of genetic engineering. Issues such as the effect of GM crops on biodiversity, the sustainability of ecosystems, the effect of GM technology on societies, economies and rural development cannot be studied in isolation or by individual countries. They can only be tackled by groups coming together and co-operating.

Timeline

1953 Publication of the proposed structure of DNA by scientists Francis Crick and James Watson

1970 Isolation of the first restriction enzyme (molecular scissors) from a bacterium by Hamilton Smith at John Hopkins University, Baltimore

1971 Development of the technique of *in vitro* fertilisation by biologists Patrick Steptoe and Robert Edwards in the UK

1972 Production of the first recombinant DNA by Janet Mertz and Ron Davis at Stanford University, California

1973 Restriction enzymes are used by Stanley Cohen and Herbert Boyer to transfer genes from one species to another

1977 Production of the first recombinant DNA containing mammalian DNA.

1978 Birth of Louise Brown in the UK, the world's first test-tube baby, conceived using IVF

1980 Birth of the first transgenic mouse

1983 Production of the first genetically modified plant (a tobacco plant) by the Mexican scientist Luis Herrera-Estrella, using a bacterium called *Agrobacterium*

1986 Birth of the first cloned sheep and first cloned cows from early embryo cells. These animals were produced by transferring a nucleus from an embryo into an egg cell

1987 Production of the first artificially insect-resistant crop plant using a gene from a bacterium which is resistant to certain insects

1990 Production of the first GM tomato which ripens more slowly and stays fresher for longer

1990 Start of the Human Genome Project involving teams of scientists around the world

1990 First use of a GMO in food is a modified yeast for bread-making

1993 Sale of GM tomatoes in the USA

1995 Birth of Morag and Megan, two cloned sheep genetically engineered to produce human drugs

1996 Birth of Dolly the sheep, the first clone of an adult mammalian cell

1996 First GM soybean and maize crops planted in North America

1997 Sale of GM food in Europe, although the food is not labelled as such

1997 Birth of Polly the sheep, a transgenic sheep that carries two human genes

1998 First cloned human cells produced by a US company called Advanced Cell Technology

1998 Birth of the first cloned transgenic cow, a calf named Victoria

1999 Destruction of GM crop trials in Europe by protestors. In 2000 some of the protestors were taken to court but found not guilty

2000 Monsanto offers vitamin A-enriched rice technology for free to improve nutrition in developing countries

2000 The US Environment Protection Agency announces publication of a report that concludes that widely used GM crops with the Bt gene offer significant benefits and few risks

2000 Announcement by Advanced Cell Technology that it is hoping to clone the extinct bucardo, a type of mountain goat once found in Spain

2000 Publication of the first working draft of the human genetic code by researchers involved with the Human Genome Project

2001 Birth of a baby gaur called Noah. Unfortunately he dies within days. The gaur is an endangered species of wild ox found in India

2001 MPs in the House of Commons vote to allow the creation of human clones for research into serious diseases

2001 Announcement by Professor Antinori, an Italian infertility specialist, that he will be ready to clone babies within the next two years

2001 Publication of the draft of the rice genome

2001 Announcement of the birth of clones of a top ranking dairy Holstein cow named Zita

2002 Mexican government admit that the valuable varieties of maize have been contaminated by GM maize

2002 Leak of European Commission report that shows that the co-existence of GM and GM crops will be technically difficult

2002 Debate continues over the release of GM salmon

2002 Approval of plans for the full labelling and traceability of genetically modified foods by the European parliament

APPENDIX

Foods which may contain genetically modified DNA, or be derived from it

GM soya	GM maize	GM tomatoes
Bread	Beer	
Confectionery	Bakery products	Tomato paste
Noodles	Salad dressing	Tomato purée
Bakery ingredients	Margarine	Tomato sauce
Biscuits	Flour	(Whole GM tomatoes are not yet approved for sale in the UK)
Cereals	Glucose syrup	
Ice cream	Corn	
Chocolate products	Corn starch	
Hydrolysed vegetable protein	Corn oil	
Soya	Modified starch	
Soya beans	Starch	
Soya flour	Corn syrup	

Global cultivation of conventional and GM crops in 2001

Crop	Total area under cultivation/million ha	Area of GM crop under cultivation/ ha	Percentage GM / %
cotton	34	6.8	20
maize (corn)	140	9.8	7
oil seed rape	25	2.7	11
soy bean	72	33.3	46
Total	271	52.6	19

Riboflavin (vitamin B2)

The Government has accepted the advice of the Advisory Committee on Novel Foods and Processes that food safety clearance should be given to riboflavin derived from genetically modified bacteria. Large quantities of the vitamin can be produced by the GM bacteria cultured in fermenters. The riboflavin is identical to that produced by traditional chemical means, and will be used to fortify processed foods such as breakfast cereals and soft drinks. The riboflavin content of the food is displayed on the label, but food manufacturers are not legally required to indicate the source of the riboflavin.

Useful Web addresses

www.bbc.co.uk (BBC news site has the latest GM stories)

http://www.geneticsforum.org.uk/index.htm (The Genetics Forum is the only independent organisation in the UK concerned with the use of new genetic technologies and their public policy implications.)

www.monsanto.co.uk (Monsanto have a comprehensive site with news stories, information on genetic research and a biotechnology knowledge centre)

www.newscientist.com (there is a special section on GM issues which covers the latest stories)

www.guardian.co.uk/gmdebate (GM stories that have appeared in the *Guardian*)

www.princeofwales.gov.uk (HRH Prince Charles' web site)

www.defra.gov.uk (website of the Department of Environment, Food and Rural Affairs)

www.nuffieldfoundation.org/bioethics (the full text of the Nuffield Council on Bioethics report 'Genetically modified crops: the ethical and social issues' is available on this site)

www.syngenta.com (Syngenta's website features information about their products and their current research)

http://www.thecampaign.org/index.html (A grassroots organisation in the US campaigning for the labelling of GM foods, with links to news stories from around the world)

Crops currently undergoing field trials in Europe or the US

Crop	Improvement
Apples	Resistance to insects
Asparagus	Male-only plants (Female asparagus plants are not suitable for eating, and usually have to be weeded out!)
Bananas	Plants that are free of viruses and worm parasites
Broccoli	Slower ripening, so flower head stays green for longer and doesn't turn yellow
Canola/ oil seed rape	Various changes in oil composition (e.g. to make unsaturated fats)
Celery/carrots	Retention of crispness, even when cut
Coffee	Better flavour, yields and pest resistance, lower caffeine content
Cabbage	Resistance to attack by caterpillars
Cucumber	Resistance to viruses, fungi and bacteria
Maize/sweetcorn	Resistance to pests
Melon	Extended shelf life of fruit
Grapes	New seedless varieties
Potato	Resistance to caterpillars and beetles. Lower fertiliser requirement Potatoes that absorb less fat on cooking (low-fat chips!)
Raspberries	Increased sugar content. Extended shelf life
Soyabean	Resistance to pests and herbicide
Sunflower	More nutritious oils with lower saturated fat content
Strawberries	Frost resistance, allowing early season production
Tomatoes	Resistance to viral diseases. Increase in yield with less chemical treatment. Slow ripening allowing development of flavour. Resistance to rotting after harvest. Lower water content. Frost resistance. Increased sugar content
Wheat	Flour more suitable for bread-making. Resistance to herbicide

Pharmaceutical products from a genetically modified source

Product	Use
blood clotting factors incl. factor VIII	haemophilia
colony stimulating factors	cancer
erthropoietin	anaemia after kidney failure
human growth hormone	dwarfism due to inactive pituitary gland
insulin	diabetes
interferons	cancers
tissue plasminogen activator	blood clots
reproductive hormones	hormone replacement therapy (HRT)
vaccines	viral infections

GM farm-scale trials — how are they set up?

During the spring of 1999, a number of farm-scale trials were established in the UK. The aim was to evaluate the impact of planting of two types of oil seed rape and one of fodder maize on the farmland wildlife.

The process that took place was as follows :

1. The government and plant breeding industry agreed to carry out farm-scale trials on three GM crops. These were intended to run for up to 4 years. The research was carried out by independent contractors funded by the Dept of Transport and Environment, MAFF, and the Scottish Office. The industry body SCIMAC (Supply Chain Initiative on Modified Agricultural Crops) provided the GM crops and liaised with farmers about evaluation sites. SCIMAC is responsible for drawing up guidelines and code of conduct.

2. The research was carried out by independent contractors. The research contracts were put out to tender. They were given to a consortium of three organisations — The Institute of Terrestrial Ecology, Institute of Arable Crop Research and the Scottish Crop Research Institute. Each institute in the consortium was responsible for one of the crops. The consortium was selected because

it proposed the best scientific methods and demonstrated the best ability to undertake a large project and they were leading experts in this field of research.

3. The research was guided by a steering committee of independent scientific experts, independent from government, the biotech industry and the contractors. They included representatives from English Nature, RSPB, and universities.

4. The steering group met with the contractors on numerous occasions and monitored the progress, advised on methods and reviewed data analysis.

5. The basic design of the experiment was to have farms on which a GM crop and non GM equivalent variety could be grown. The abundance and diversity of the wildlife was monitored and compared.

6. The crop was grown following normal farm practice. The field size was similar to that used on commercial farms.

As a result of widespread damage to the crops by protestors, much of the 1999 research was invalidated. As a consequence, there is no evidence to show whether GM crops will or will not harm farm wildlife.

GLOSSARY

amino acid: the building blocks of proteins, proteins are made up of a chain of amino acids joined together. There are 20 naturally occurring amino acids, including eight so-called essential amino acids which cannot be made by the human body and have to be obtained in the diet.

antibiotic: a drug that kills or inhibits the growth of harmful bacteria. As antibiotics are used more widely, bacteria are becoming resistant to these drugs.

antibodies : chemicals made by white blood cells to destroy disease-causing organisms which have invaded the body and other foreign substances.

asthma: a respiratory disease. The sufferer experiences difficulty in breathing when exposed to certain substances or conditions.

atom: the tiniest part of a substance.

biotechnology: the use of plant and animal cells, micro-organisms such as bacteria and fungi, viruses and their products, to produce useful substances.

chemotherapy: drug treatment given to cancer patients which kills the cancer cells.

chromosome: one of the thread-like structures in a nucleus, made up of DNA and protein. Chromosomes become visible during cell division. Each chromosome may carry many different genes. There are 23 pairs of chromosomes in a human cell, except in red blood cells which have no chromosomes and the sex cells. Sex cells (sperm and egg) are produced in a special kind of cell division which halves the chromosome number. They have 23 single chromosomes.

clone: an individual that is identical with one or more other individuals.

DNA: deoxyribonucleic acid. The molecule that carries the genetic code.

DNA probe: a short length of DNA which is used to detect a gene to which the probe can bind.

DNA sequence: the exact order of bases (cytosine, guanine, thymine and adenine) along a DNA strand.

embryo: a plant or animal as it develops from a fertilised egg.

enzyme: a biological catalyst, made of protein, that is able to catalyse (increase the speed of) reactions within living organisms.

fertilisation: the joining together of a male and female sex cell to form a new individual.

genome: the complete set of genes carried by a sex cell.

gene: a unit of inheritance that is passed on from parent to offspring. Each gene is made of a length of DNA.

gene therapy: the treatment of genetic disorders by repairing damaged genes or introducing new ones.

genetic code: the sequence of chemical bases in DNA which code for specific amino acids.

genetic modification: the production of new combinations of genetic material by altering the DNA of an organism. Usually a gene from one organism is introduced into the DNA of another.

heredity: genetic transmission from generation to generation.

hormone: a chemical messenger, produced by special glands, which controls the various bodily activities, for example adrenalin and insulin.

human genome project: the huge international project to map the location of every gene on human chromosomes and to work out the entire genetic code.

immune system: the natural defence system which protects the body against infection by disease-causing organisms.

molecule: a group of atoms bonded together.

mutation: a sudden change in genetic information from one generation to another. When cells divide the DNA is copied very accurately. But very occasionally mistakes are made. Sometimes the error can be harmful and it causes a genetic disorder, but often it remains unnoticed or is even beneficial. A gene mutation results from the change in the sequence of bases in the DNA, causing a change in the genetic code. Chromosome mutations are caused by lengths of chromosome becoming detached, lost or duplicated.

plasmid: a small circular length of DNA found in the cytoplasm of bacterial cells and which is used in genetic engineering.

protein: a large molecule made from amino acids. It is important for growth and repair. Protein-rich foods include meat, dairy produce, eggs and fish.

toxin: a poison produced by a living organism.

transgenic: describes an organism containing genetic material artificially inserted from another species.

virus: a strand of DNA or RNA surrounded by protein which can only reproduce by invading a living cell.

INDEX